SOUL
AMONG
LIONS

SOUL AMONG LIONS

THE COUGAR AS PEACEFUL ADVERSARY

Harley Shaw

The University of Arizona Press
Tucson

DEDICATED TO
Chink, Rattler, and Moonshine

The University of Arizona Press
© 1994 Harley G. Shaw
First University of Arizona Press paperbound edition 2000
All rights reserved

www.uapress.arizona.edu

Library of Congress Cataloging-in-Publication Data
Shaw, Harley G.
Soul among lions : the cougar as peaceful adversary / Harley Shaw.
1st University of Arizona Press paperbound ed.
p. cm.
Originally published: Boulder : Johnson Books, c1989.
ISBN 0-8165-2084-4 (pbk.)
1. Pumas. I. Title.
QL737.C23 S52 2000
599.75'24—dc21
00-041154

Manufactured in the United States of America on acid-free,
archival-quality paper.

15   14   13   12   11   10   7   6   5   4   3   2

Contents

Introduction to the New Paperbound Edition

Regarding mountain lion populations, little has changed since this book was first published. Given adequate habitat, the species is resilient. Some folks say lion numbers are increasing in the West, but no wildlife agency has found a practical way to count them. With the exception of a few research areas, population estimates for lions remain guesses.

Lion taxonomy has changed. Molecular geneticists, comparing DNA from populations across North and South America, reduced subspecies from thirty-two to six. In North America the number dropped from fourteen to one. Also, the scientific name has changed. The lion is now *Puma concolor.* I would like to see *puma* become the accepted common name. It is short and easy to spell, and it recognizes the cat's unique New World origins. I now stubbornly use it in my writings.

In Arizona and California, political pressures for puma control have increased. These pressures come less from ranchers than from hunters and wildlife biologists. Ranchers, struggling for economic survival on western rangelands, now see pumas as only a very small part of their problems. As always, many hunters would reduce predator numbers to produce more deer, and some biologists now worry about puma predation on scattered populations of desert bighorn sheep. These issues will probably always be recycled. The puma has withstood both sport hunting and control efforts for more than a century. Given adequate habitat, it will continue to do so.

People who hunt pumas or seek their control are at least aware of the species and value the wildlands where it lives. Now, even more than before, I see the loss of space caused by those oblivious to wildlands as the greatest threat to pumas. I believe that such people are the majority in our money-hungry culture. The loss and fragmentation of habitat through urbanization has become the new environmental demon in the West, as well it should. Golf courses for wealthy retirees, large homes (often second homes) plastered on hillsides, and the humble ranchettes of edge-dwelling workers all displace populations of pumas and their prey. Housing starts, reported daily in the news, are a major indicator of our economic well-being. We have no similar daily report of ecological well-being.

But urbanization is only the visible part of our society's increasing effects on habitat. Every new car, every item of food, every book we buy comes ultimately from resources produced on the land, a fact ignored by economic indices. Their production requires space. We seldom see the habitats that are destroyed to provide our toys. Clear linkages between the Dow Jones Industrial Average and the remaining puma habitat are difficult to establish, but I have little doubt that an inverse relationship exists between the two. I'm always disappointed when I meet a wildlife biologist who is "well invested."

Twenty years ago I climbed Mount Trumbull with a companion and, looking over the vast, empty landscape of the Arizona Strip, spontaneously poured forth my disillusionment with wildlife agencies. That mountaintop epiphany became part of this book; the companion became my wife. We now climb a small hill behind our house in Chino Valley and monitor the subdivision of grasslands and the growth of "starter castles" on the juniper-covered slopes of Yavapai County. We experience no epiphany, only despair.

Not too long ago, however, I climbed this hill with a young German engineer who has a special love for the American Western. As I sat bemoaning the crowded landscape below us, Peter shook his head and said, "I don't understand." I asked him to elaborate. He pointed out to me that Germany is similar in land area to Arizona, yet it has a population of 80 million people. Arizona has less than 5 million. Where I saw a crowded landscape, he saw vast open space. Germany and most other European countries have had high population densities for centuries. Their large carnivores were extirpated over much of their range before 1800.

For wildlands and wild species, the western United States is now at a point reached by Europe centuries ago. We still have expanses of undeveloped landscapes, and most of our large carnivores, though reduced in distribution, still exist. At the same time, we know infinitely more about the habitat needs of wild species than did our ancestors in the Middle Ages. We have a growing environmental ethic, and we seemingly still have a choice in the matter. The question, of course, is whether we as a culture care enough about wildlife to improve upon the Old World's record. Or, perhaps, whether we can modify our behavior even if we do care. Let us hope that we are not, as some now say, destined by our genes to reproduce obsessively, buy more gadgets, build more houses, and eliminate the territories of creatures that compete with our immediate needs. If so, no matter what our technological accomplishments, we will remain just another mammalian species, controlled by instinct and incapable of moral growth.

Foreword

One could not have picked a better place for the Third Mountain Lion Workshop than Prescott, Arizona. The town not only sprawls over into some of the West's most famous lion country, but like America's biggest cat, Prescott's transition into the eighties has been an uneasy one. Recently renowned mostly as a rodeo and retirement burg, Prescott is now a bustling mixture of Stetsons and down vests, boutiques, and Mother Earth News.

For three days in December, biologists and wildlife managers from ten states and two Canadian provinces presented their research, summarized what they knew about the lion's status, and pondered the animal's future. Ranchers, hunters, naturalists, predator control agents, and government administrators were among the almost two hundred people in attendance. It seemed that anyone who had ever touched a mountain lion was there, along with more than a few who never had and never would.

One of those who had was Harley Shaw. It was he who had organized the symposium. Harley did not give a paper, preferring instead to facilitate the proceedings and listen to the accomplishments of others. Not that Harley did not have much to say, he knows as much about lions as anyone. It is just that he knows too much to tell it all at one sitting.

Harley conducted not one but two lion research studies in Arizona, on the Spider and Cross U ranches northwest of Prescott and on the Kaibab plateau. More recently, he and his crews completed a statewide lion survey that not only studied each major lion habitat, but also looked at such far-flung lion haunts as the Sand Tank Mountains on the Barry Goldwater Gunnery Range and Mount Trumbull on the Arizona Strip. He has been living and thinking mountain lions for almost twenty years. Lions are his passion. To write a book about his lion experiences is as natural for Harley as it was for Hemingway to write about Spain.

Harley's book is about much more than mountain lion biology, although the reader will find enough of that to whet even the most latent taste for natural history. Personalities and philosophies are as much a part of Harley's story as hounds and horses. All of us who care enough about mountain lioins to have an opinion about them are included somewhere in the text. Ranchers, conservationists, and agency administrators will all find more to like in this book than to agree with.

Whether you are a hunter or not, whether you hate lions, love them, or are somewhere in between, Harley's book will make you think. Such is the power of all good books. And this is a very good book indeed.

David E. Brown
Author of *The Wolf in the Southwest, The Grizzly in the Southwest,* and a variety of other books

Preface

Several years ago, I was invited to speak on mountain lions at a Rocky Mountain Lyceum in Estes Park, Colorado. Since leaving the Arizona Game and Fish Department in 1990, I had given few public presentations on lions. I found it too easy to fall back into the role of research biologist representing an agency—a role I could no longer honestly assume.

In accepting the Estes Park engagement, I was gambling that four years absence from the game department had provided the distance I needed to speak my own mind. I was right, but I was surprised at my words. I found myself speaking not about lions, but of land use and the importance of saving the grand spaces that we call the West. The lion had become only a symbol of a greater problem, and the issues that I had once thought important—hunting, preservationism, predator control, ranching—became insignificant in the face of current losses of habitat.

Insofar as I know, hunting or trapping have never extirpated a mountain lion population. Nor has total protection ever permanently saved one. The eastern cougar ceased to exist when human densities on the land reached a point where cougars could no longer avoid encounters with humans, their livestock, or their dogs. Bullets may well have been decimating agents as cougars, state by state, ceased to exist. But it was large numbers of people scattered across the land that made it impossible for the eastern cats to avoid the bullets.

Modern radio-tracking studies support this hypothesis. They have demonstrated repeatedly that established resident mountain lions do not abandon their home areas because of human disturbance. Animals captured and released a half dozen times or more continue to return to their established routines. Studies on the Florida panther and on lions in the Santa Ana Mountains of California both demonstrate that increasing human densities, associated loss of habitat and connective corridors, and ultimate conflict with human settlement are the forces destroying mountain lions.

We still have lions in the West, because we still have enough habitat. Throughout my years of work on the lion, the vastness of western landscapes and the existence of large expanses of public land left me complacent regarding the fate of the lion. I worried little about the effects of hunting or predator control. As long as we had adequate space, these remained moral issues, with little significance to the continued existence of lions. Their main value lay in keeping quixotic individuals occupied in meetings and away from the land.

But I am now worried about the effects of human encroachment, and I believe that the West is now experiencing the same phenomenon that decimated the cougar in the East. As *Puma concolor* (now, so I'm told, the official scientific name of the mountain lion) disappeared east of the Mississippi, we were left with a fairly extensive lore of lion attacks on humans. Such stories were so common that some early writers suggested that the eastern cat was naturally more aggressive than our western subspecies. I don't think so. I believe that the incidence of attacks in the East was directly related to the increase of humans on the land. I also believe that, as people continue to move into cougar habitat in the West, we are seeing more of the same thing here. Over the past ten years, encounters between humans and cougars have increased. Attacks, near misses, and a few fatalities have occurred. This is not a result of changes in cougars. They are still living and eating in their established ranges, as we know they will do. But human densities and forms of human land use have changed.

In the midst of battles over grazing, logging, and hunting, often carried out by people living on small rural acreages, we have failed to acknowledge that the single most destructive force affecting large carnivores is our own presence on the land. Most of us move into the country because we love wildlife; we want to live close to nature. But none of us will tolerate having our pets or children eaten. We won't tolerate even the slightest chance. When lion/human encounters occur, the lion (or bear, or wolf) always ultimately loses.

In his 1933 text on wildlife management, Aldo Leopold classified some species as wilderness animals—creatures that could not live close to humans. The lion, the grizzly, the wolf all fell into this category. In most cases they fit this class not because they couldn't tolerate humans, but because humans couldn't tolerate them. Such creatures need vast expanses of habitat where they can avoid people.

But how much habitat? I'm not sure, but I think we may now begin to guess. Modern conservation biologists have estimated the population size required to sustain the genetic diversity of a species over the long haul. With various safety factors built in, this usually comes out to be about 500 breeding animals. I sincerely hope we never get down to this low number for mountain lions, but it gives us a basis for calculating minimum habitat needs. Using densities of lions observed in various studies in the western U.S., we might conjecture that the *minimum* area of habitat needed to sustain 500 breeding lions would be about 10,000 square miles (6.4 million acres). This assumes high prey densities and suitable habitat throughout the area. If we calculate for a more likely scenario, where prey and lions must move between seasonal ranges, or where prey and habitat are irregularly distributed, we must multiply our habitat estimate by a factor of two or three. On the order of 30,000 square miles (almost 20 million acres) is more realistic. This is an area about 175 miles on a side.

We may not even now have a single block of lion habitat of that size remaining in the West. In fact, we may never have had. Certainly all of western landscapes did not support lions. But we do have sizable chunks of unsettled land, and, if corridors connecting these areas can be sustained to allow the various populations to genetically interconnect, we can have lions for a long, long time. But if the corridors are closed, we may see more and more of what happened to the eastern cougar, and what is happening to the Florida panther and to the lions in the California's Santa Ana Mountains. Unfortunately, the lands that form these corridors in the West—valley bottoms and foothills—are largely private, hence vulnerable to residential development.

Our two greatest problems lie in thinking on such a large scale and bringing ourselves to attack the sanctity of private lands. Based upon what we now know about movements of transient animals, lions in the western United States probably should be considered a single interconnected population. Saving corridors of habitat for such a mobile species would require land use planning at a level not attempted since John Wesley Powell tried unsuccessfully to organize the West. Westerners themselves would have to rethink the way they live.

I'm not optimistic. Our wildlife agencies have repeatedly demonstrated inability to overcome territoriality and political anxieties in time to deal with large-scaled controversial issues. Politicians and lay game commissioners are too ignorant of the complexities of modern biology to make wise decisions. Private citizens have no history and no current incentives to limit their life styles for the benefit of wildlife. While legally restricting use of private land attacks the very roots of our American way of life, developers have massive financial incentive to keep developing. I doubt seriously that even our public lands will be sacrosanct once the private acreages are all occupied by buildings. In view of human history in other places and of accelerating expansionism in the West, I predict that conservationists (including agriculturists, hunters, and preservationists) will continue to fiddle with inconsequential and divisive issues while the landscapes around us are consumed. At current rates of human population growth, I expect that the wild mountain lion will be present through my lifetime. My grandchildren will remember it existed. My great-grandchildren may find it difficult to discern lion history from bison history as they interact with "nature" on their multi-media entertainment centers.

Acknowledgments

Within the Arizona Game and Fish Department, Steve Gallizioli gave early staff-level support to lion research. I'm particularly grateful to him for hanging with me after that first lion-less winter. Ron Smith and Dave Roe also gave strong Phoenix-based support to the project and listened to my cries of anguish when fiscal matters moved too slowly for me.

In the field, Norm Woolsey provided the level of technical expertise that made the Spider Ranch study succeed. His even, congenial manner was instrumental in keeping us on course, and his basic field skills made all the difference. Long, tedious hours afield, wild, uncooperative dogs, and stubborn horses couldn't fluster him.

Lou Cox contributed similar support and expertise and gave us badly needed relief each summer. He also demonstrated that snares were another method of capturing lions.

And of course, George Goswick was the key element in our work on the Spider. His easy approach to handling dogs, patience with our inexperience, and dry humor were second in importance only to his ability to catch lions. He unselfishly helped us start our own pack.

Bill Workman filled in several times when George was unavailable. He, too, provided good dogs and good days in the woods. Clell Lee and Dale Lee each helped catch cats and added to our lore of the lion, as did Bill Murphy and Ollie Barney. We learned something from each of them.

Eugene P. Polk of Prescott, Arizona, first offered use of the Spider and Cross U Ranches for a study area. He provided housing, horses, and at times, vehicles. He maintained a liberal attitude toward involvement of his ranch personnel and had a calming influence when misunderstandings between the private sector (cowboys) and the public sector (biologists) arose.

Margaret T. Morris of Spider Ranch also provided use of

housing and equipment. She is most memorable for the mixture of good conversation, Guiness Stout, and Coors that she provided at the end of a few long work days.

Louis Barassi and the late Edward Steele were instrumental in acquiring a grant from the Defenders of Wildlife during our first year at Spider Ranch. These funds gave the study a badly needed impetus as we learned how expensive radio-tracking lions could really be.

On the Kaibab, Bill Powers provided good-natured assistance through two of the wettest winters on record. Few people can find humor in three stuck pickups and a runaway horse, but Bill managed to find a way. Norris Dodd took Bill's place during the last year and adapted quickly to the job. He survived twelve months with a disgruntled biologist who might have convinced a less dedicated person that any business in the world was better than agency work.

Priscilla Steinhauer, too, endured two long winters on the Kaibab and interrupted her life goals for that period. She tried for seven years to understand the obsessions of a field biologist.

Patty Woodruff and David E. Brown have been the main forces pushing me to finish this manuscript. Their encouragement and comments essentially brought it to completion. Charles Bowden, Sally Antrobus, Susan Morse, Virginia Fifield, and Jay Dusard all commented on the manuscript, and their suggestions have improved it in many places.

Introduction

A reviewer of an early draft of this manuscript noted an inconsistency in the name I gave its subject. I used cougar to deal with the abstract, generalized, or mystical beast and reserved mountain lion or simply lion for the tangible critter we fitted with radios and followed around. At the time of writing I was not conscious of the distinction but could see it clearly as I revised the book. I decided to retain it as consistently as possible. As a result, in the body of the manuscript, I've used the name that is common in Arizona, where I worked. For most of this book, we'll talk of mountain lions. I reserve cougar for the generalization.

That I had unconsciously developed a distinction is important, because it demonstrates differences in the ways that species can be viewed. Cougar and mountain lion are simply two regional common names for the animal known as *Felis concolor* in scientific literature. For a houndsman in Utah or Idaho, the term cougar has no special significance. It means the same thing that mountain lion means to me. However, over a period of years, cougar had come to represent a gestalt of lion which was something more than the morphological cat.

This distinction stems from the fact that closeness to a species modifies the way we perceive it. Early in a study, we try to isolate our subject and view it as a single, simple entity. In my college ecology classes, as I remember, this was called autecology. In it, we look at morphology, physiology, genetics, behavior, or any other grouping of characteristics that would render an organism finite. But autecology becomes impossible. As soon as you investigate morphology, for example, you must view its adaptive values. This leads you into both ancient and current environments of the species. Physiological studies likewise lead to assessment of food and energy balances—and assessment of the environment. Genetics, behavior, all traits of an animal, require environmental awareness for their full understanding. The species inevitably comes out as only a small part of a system, a community.

Species cannot, then, be defined within their morphological bounds. A species includes the animal itself plus its habitat, its food, and its behavioral interactions with other organisms. The term *umwelt* (German for environment) is used to describe this and in its most liberal form includes the history of the whole universe in the makeup of every species. Thus "cougar" had unconsciously formed in my mind to denote the *umwelt* of the mountain lion.

I'd like to let the distinction stand in hopes of trying to convey this broader concept of cougar as it formed within me during the past fifteen years. I know this is overly ambitious, for, based upon this notion, all living species exist at a focal point of evolution. Each species is a product of eons, physically, genetically, culturally. In a sense, a species is an equal sign in time, focusing all of the evolutionary forces that molded it into the present and channeling them into an as yet unspecified result in the future. In trying to understand the nature of the cougar, I found that I could trace each of the historical components backward only a tiny distance. They were not only poorly documented; they converged, crossed, intermingled, and influenced each other. I could not see the future side of the equation at all, hence was left with a concept of cougar based upon a vague understanding of the ephemeral present.

So, however grandiose my goals for this book, I'm really stuck with talking about lions and the factors influencing them over the past few decades. These are mostly human-induced factors created by a variety of interest groups, each with its own collective concept of cougar. These varied perspectives and their influence on society will probably determine the fate of the lion. We need to understand all of them in order to acquire any vision of the future. But we can assess them only as they relate to biological reality here and now.

Delineating this reality is the goal of biologists doing research, and, like any other occupation, research is attended by its own practical problems. To succeed in research, scientists must sustain an image of objectivity. Critical peers and journal editors do not condone vague notions, feelings, or opinions. Data and well-based conclusions are the legitimate currency of professional scientists, and publication of data ensures employment.

In order to publish, we as biologists must separate the objective wheat from the subjective chaff. Considering the difficulties involved in gathering data on unwilling wild subjects, and the cumbersomeness of field logistics, especially when working on low-density wilderness species such as the lion, the amount of wheat is very often disproportionately small. For many of us, this becomes a source of frustration. At the end of a study, we display a few facts, but we seldom disclose the truth. The story of the work, the feelings we developed, the overall knowledge and skills we gained, are necessarily discounted in deference to hard-core data. Yet I think this so-called chaff is also important. The scientist's own visions of personal accomplishment, conceptualizations of the subject studied, and feelings for that subject are levels of knowledge that could influence political or managerial decisions and direct future studies. Too often, this level of knowledge is buried as the researcher leaves one area of endeavor and enters a new one.

The process is unfair both to the scientist and to the community that supports research. It doesn't allow researchers to clear their mental load before moving on, and it leaves interpretation to popularizers who cannot attain the scientist's depth of perception. The results are misunderstanding and misinterpretation. Yet neither humans nor the species being studied can realize the full benefit of new information until the scientist's thoughts are in some way generalized and become part of collective knowledge. Under the best of circumstances, this takes time.

In sustaining our image of objectivity, we as biologists pretend that we study wild animals. In reality, we inevitably study an interface between ourselves and other species, and we in fact often lose sight of the distinction between domesticity and wildness. We enter a study with knowledge of the technical literature, information from popular media, advice from peers, and our own previous experience. We approach our subject as if it were an alien being. As we gather new data, we begin to lose preconceptions and rely more upon our own senses. Inevitably, we modify not only our knowledge of the species being studied; we modify our feelings for it, for our previous sources of information, and for ourselves as well. At some point, we each become unique in our knowledge and judge our mentors and our culture from this unique point of view. In a sense, we come to view our own species from the perspective of the species we study, and that species no longer seems particularly alien or wild.

Research thus becomes a process of personal change as we become involved with our subject. Some species create more change than others. Small, noncontroversial creatures will cause little stress. They provide peaceful areas of endeavor that are good for the stable soul. With a large predator, however, the excitement begins. Not only is the animal itself stimulating, its highly polarized human constituencies will bludgeon you with their respective points of view and will bruise you emotionally. You will repeatedly be forced to reexamine your beliefs, and you will find them constantly questioned by others. You will grow and adjust, or you will leave the arena. Objectivity becomes difficult.

These ideas, then, set the tone of this book. It is in large part chaff; the afterbirth of research. It is about mountain lions and mountain lion prey, in part. It is also about human attitudes toward the lion and how these attitudes, and the conflicts they create, relate to information that recent research has provided. Finally, because of my involvement with the lion, the book is also about a dissociation I've come to feel with my own species and about my growing disillusionment with its self-centered attitudes. By getting so close to such a controversial animal, I have begun to dislike the way humans view themselves. This has inevitably developed as an underlying theme of the book, much as it developed within me as an unexpected result of research.

Nonetheless, I am still human, and I must write from human perspectives. The reader will sense that I waver between the viewpoints of the biologist and the hunter. These are the handles by which I grasped the cougar, and they are not greatly different from each other. Whether one seeks a trophy or a fact, one must hunt. Although killing is not the goal in research, dogs, snares, and guns (tranquilizer)—adaptations of the hunter's tools—are used to capture and mark the animals. Stalking and reading of sign are used to gather data after the cats are marked. Hence, although biologists seek information rather than pelts, we nonetheless hunt, and the skills we develop and refine are those of the hunter. I relied upon the sensitivities and skills of experienced lion hunters to develop my concept of cougar. As a result, I have an irrational prejudice that is perhaps inconsistent with my present view of lions: I find it hard to envision them existing in the absence of hounds.

Other prejudices exist. Ranchers and preservationists have opposing concepts of cougar. They both will certainly affect the future of the species. Deer hunters are generally not lion hunters, except by accident. They, too, view the species differently, and they will influence the politics of cougar. Trophy hunters being guided for lions place a totally different value upon the cat than does the lay houndsman, for example, trying to reach his first tree, and the professional guide has a different view than either of these. Conservation and land management agencies, while abstractions in themselves, are made up of professionals who presumably manage lions and their habitat. Within the ranks of these professionals, however, differences exist. Goals in management vary from agency to agency and from level to level within agencies. Because the human species seems for the present to be in control of this planet, the attitudes of these different groups will collectively affect the future of cougar. Much of this book will assess the attitudes of these various groups and attempt to determine how these attitudes mesh with the best known facts.

THE
COUGAR
COMPONENT

CHAPTER ONE
A Place of Birth

 The smallest kittens I've seen in the wild were barely nine days old. Their eyes had just begun to open. In retrospect, I've realized that this incident was probably the only time I came close to being attacked by a lion, and that, possibly, only a whole series of accidents prevented such an attack from happening.

I was not looking specifically for kittens at the time. One of our radioed females had not moved for more than a week, and we needed to know why. Normally, failure of a lion to change places for two or three successive days indicated it was feeding on an animal it had killed, and we would attempt to identify its prey. In this case, something, perhaps observations of other radioed lions, had prevented us from entering the area sooner. After nine days of immobility, however, this cat took priority. Such extended immobility suggested either a dead lion or a slipped collar. We were uneasy about what we would find.

The beep of the radio was emanating from the head of a steep, brushy canyon on the west-facing slope of Cottonwood Mountain, probably the largest mountain mass in the Spider Ranch study area. During aerial tracking, we had not been able to tell whether the signal came from the rimrock along the walls of the canyon or from the canyon bottom. The hand-held loop antenna we used on the ground actually gave us little better information. Even with the help of directional radio equipment, we still had to grid the area on foot.

We had brought my strike dog Chink and a young bluetick called Moonshine but opted to leave them at the truck during the initial search. I really had no reason to tree the cat, and I hoped to see it, if it was alive, without the use of dogs. Norm Woolsey, the other half of the research team, was to stay at the truck and bring the hounds if needed. We tied the dogs in the shade of two large Emory oaks. The August heat, nearing the hundred-degree mark, would have killed them in short order had we left them inside the vehicle.

I climbed the north ridge along the steep canyon, checking my receiver every hundred yards or so for changes in signal strength or direction. Within minutes I was sweating and hoping the search would be short. Climbing Arizona mountains in August, even at six thousand feet, can dehydrate one rapidly.

As I approached the head of the canyon, the signal strengthened from the well-defined musical beep to a flat, loud thump. Such a signal said I was so close that the loop antenna was saturated. It would give me little help in locating the lion beyond this point. I was probably within a hundred yards of the animal. Using my body and larger rocks along the canyon wall, I experimented with screening the antenna and concluded that the strongest signal, amidst all of the rebounds and echoes, came more or less from the south. This placed the lion either in the rimrock on the far rim of the canyon or in the thick brush in the bottom. The brush prevented sighting the lion if it was at the bottom, so I focused my initial attention on the far ledges.

From the shade of a large basalt boulder, I glassed every detail of the far slope, hoping that I'd be lucky enough to spot the cat. I knew the odds were against me. Few animals are harder to see. After a half-hour with binoculars, I gave up. As a last-ditch effort, before moving out into the sun again, I fired a shot from my .357 handgun into a nearby dirt bank and once more glassed the far side of the canyon. The sound of the shot hadn't disturbed the cat if it was present. I saw nothing but the movements of towhees in the chaparral. I heard Chink break into a wild, chopping bark far below me at the truck. I could not understand his excitement at gunshots. He had never been used in killing lions, and his only experience with anything resembling firearms was the air pistol we used to propel tranquilizer darts. Its pneumatic thump was only faintly similar to the crack of a true firearm. Yet somehow Chink connected guns with game, and the sound of a shot sent him into a frenzy. I had at times used my pistol to signal him off of a track that we, for some reason, had chosen not to follow.

4

Rather than lose my hard-earned elevation, I decided to work on around the head of the canyon to the far side before dropping into the bottom. In the intense August heat, I avoided any extra expenditure of energy and went downhill only when necessary. Also, by circling the signal, I would learn more about its origin.

Even before I reached the far rim, I was convinced that the pulse was coming from the scrub oak thicket in the bottom of the draw. On the faint hope that I might yet move the cat, I discharged another shot into a safe bank, but the radio signal remained unchanged. I suspected by this time that I was dealing with a dead animal or a slipped collar.

At my second shot, Chink again opened below. As I started working my way down the steep slope, I realized that he was changing location. His bark grew louder, and within minutes, I could see him following my track up the far canyon wall. Even in the heat, he had taken a scant ten minutes to trail me up a slope I had spent nearly an hour in climbing.

Norm had apparently taken my shots as signals to release the dogs and come to me. Chink rapidly joined me, and I soon spotted Norm slowly climbing. Moonshine, being young and inexperienced, stayed close to Norm. Chink and I settled into the shade of a cliff to wait. If there was lion scent in the area, Chink gave no sign. Either the lion was gone, or the extreme heat was destroying all scent. Considering the amount of disturbance I had created, along with Chink's lack of reaction, I gave up hope of seeing the cat.

When Norm arrived, I relinquished the shade to him and began to push my way into the thicket. Norm held Moonshine with a short leash. I had to force my way through the brush, pulling branches apart as I searched the ground ahead of me, expecting to see the shed radio-collar at any moment. I had ruled out the possibility of a dead lion; there was no smell. In this heat, the stench of a nine-day-old carcass should be permeating the canyon.

Chink fell in behind me, panting heavily in the heat and showing no interest in scent. I had barely covered a third of the distance through the thicket, however, when Chink suddenly roared and pushed past me into the thick brush. I had been so intent looking for the collar that I'd forgotten to look for the cat.

At the instant Chink passed me, the lion rose a scant ten feet ahead, feigned a dash in my direction, then retreated in front of the charging dog. I froze, uncertain what to do, and quickly lost sight of the cat in the thicket.

Norm released Moonshine in the excitement, and the blue dog joined us. Moonshine always had a unique personality, being independent and somewhat methodical even as a pup. He seldom reacted to the excitement of other dogs, preferring to explore the cause of the disturbance before deciding whether to join in a particular melee. He proceeded carefully around the thicket while Chink barked steadily at the far edge.

Norm informed me that the cat was pacing the hillside just above the brush across the draw. Chink was holding her at bay, but she refused to leave the area and gave signs of wanting to reenter the thicket. "I'll tell you if she starts back in," he called as he moved to a better vantage point. "Be careful."

Moonshine suddenly opened down the draw in the thickest clump of brush. Chink abandoned his sentry post and rushed to the younger dog—a move not to my liking. I really preferred that he stay between me and the cat. The lion, however, held its position.

Chink immediately signaled the cause of the new ruckus. He tucked his tail between his legs and came straight to me. I had punished him on two occasions when he had threatened orphaned kittens that I'd held at home. He remembered, and his actions made it clear he didn't intend to be spanked over the youngsters Moonshine had found. Moonshine was still too young to attack the litter. He kept his distance from them and maintained his excited puppy bark.

There were three spotted kittens, barely eight inches long, excluding their tails. They were huddled together in the debris and dead leaves under the dense crown of several shrub oaks, well protected from the sun and from potential enemies. Only one of them had begun to open its eyes.

I chose not to handle them, although weights and measurements would have been interesting. Such measurements could come from zoos. Our disturbance had already been more than enough, and I merely wanted to catch the dogs and move away before a kitten was killed. I was afraid that the mother might abandon them due to the disturbance we had already created.

Norm had kept me informed on the female's movements while I was in the thicket. She had finally moved out of sight up a small side draw. The thump on our receiver, however, told us that she was nearby.

Our radio locations from the air over the next few days indicated that the lion had returned to the "nest." Her movements gradually began to extend outward from the brushy draw, but they seemed to center around the site for another two or three weeks. From that time, movements plotted with the radio equipment and aircraft resembled more and more her movements prior to birth of the kittens. This site, apparently, was the birthplace of the young lions. It is the only such site I've examined. I've seen three other litters that may have been small enough to be in their place of birth. I was not sure, however, in any of these cases. Two of these three were in thickets; the third was in a boulder pile with much brush as well as many small caves in the surrounding rocks. I think that the nature of these locations disputes one popular misconception regarding lions. Time and again, we hear stories of lions killing rabbits and bringing them to kittens in a den. We even see movies, staged with tame lions, of these events. The den is always a cave. Popular myth holds that even when without young, lions maintain dens central to their territories. Such is simply not the case. I am not saying that lions will never have young in a cave. Certain rock overhangs surrounded by brush would be ideal birthing sites. Adult lions, however, have no home cave that they return to to produce offspring. They select a suitably protected site, be it cave or thicket, within their home area and bear kittens. By the time the kittens are weaned, they may be moved to one or more additional sites. The mother will begin to lead them to kills at an early age, perhaps seven to eight weeks.

Thus kittens learn early to move around their range and not imprint upon a single home site. Home is the entire area of use. Within it, lions are free to move, hunt, and rest as their mood and physiology directs. They are not handicapped by the human compulsion to return to a single safe base at night. Home is a large tract of land that they undoubtedly come to know as you and I know the floorplan of our house. They learn to be lions in this home area.

CHAPTER TWO
Growing Up

 There were times during the years that we meddled in the affairs of lions that I questioned the value of it all. While watching a prime male cat progress from a snarling, aggressive predator to a drooling, wide-eyed sot, then to a convulsing invalid, all because of drugs that I had injected, I wondered if hunters didn't give the animals more dignity by simply shooting them.

This problem was especially acute in studying very young kittens. We worried daily that our dogs, who definitely viewed our efforts as sport, not research, would trail into a small litter and kill all of the young. We know this happened at least once. Female lions go rapidly back into their reproductive processes when they lose a litter, so such losses were not devastating to the lion population. They did, perhaps, influence our results. We tried very hard to learn from such events so that the assets of knowledge gained could be charged against any liabilities on the species.

The story that follows is about such an event, undoubtedly the worst that happened during the study. In retrospect, I'm not sure that we could have done anything different considering our level of knowledge at the time. We did, perhaps, learn some things about lions that we would not have learned under more positive circumstances.

George Goswick was our principal hunter at Spider Ranch, a 175-square-mile area that was the site of our first five years of lion research. George was a third-generation lion hunter. His grandfather and father before him ran dogs in the wildernesses of Arizona and Texas. Giles, George's father, was perhaps the most famous lion hunter ever to hit Arizona. He hunted lions for forty years in the Verde Valley and Prescott area. George grew up following Giles and the hounds. He has instincts that many of us who started with dogs late in life will never acquire.

A few days before our story starts, George had responded to the report of a lion-killed calf on a ranch north of the Spider study area. Spider Ranch was closed to the killing of lions, and the owners had agreed to absorb all losses of cattle while the study progressed. Neighboring ranchers were not as generous, however, and according to his tradition, George attempted to kill lions that were eating beef. In this case, he had not caught the offending lion but, on a return trip through the study area, had noticed tracks of a female with three kittens. He recognized the opportunity to capture and mark a family group and contacted me.

A storm prevented us from moving into the area right away, but the five-inch layer of fresh snow it left created ideal conditions for tracking. We found tracks of the family before we left our vehicles. The mother cat with three kittens had crossed the main road running north from Camp Wood. It seemed fate was with us. We unloaded horses and dogs and set out on the track. We had limited our pack to a couple of reliable dogs, Chink and Speed, and two or three young ones that were in training. The fresh track in the snow was no challenge to the hounds, and they were soon running it at full speed. We kept the horses at a trot to stay in hearing. The chase was a short one, and within a half hour or so, we could hear dogs barking treed.

We arrived upon a classic scene: the hounds under a moderately large ponderosa pine with the female on one of its lower limbs, the kittens scattered in the limbs of smaller trees nearby, and the carcass of a partially eaten mule deer doe on the ground. We tied the dogs to protect the kittens and darted the female. Unfortunately, we were at an interim in project funding and had no radio collar, so we fitted her with a rope collar and numbered neck tag. We did not handle the kittens. Our best estimate for their age put them at about two months. They were still spotted and weighed eight to ten pounds.

We returned the next day without dogs to be sure the cat had recovered. She was gone, but the kittens were still at the capture site. Enough of the doe carcass remained to feed the youngsters, so we felt that they were secure for a day or so. Checks of the site for the next four days showed no sign of the female and a gradual decline in the condition of the young. They did not wander from the vicinity of the kill, even though it rapidly disappeared. On the fifth day after the marking of the female, I, my fourteen-year-old daughter, Jean; the ranch foreman, Bill Murphy; his wife, Pat; and his son, Billy, all returned to the site. The female still had not returned, so we gathered the kittens into gunny sacks and took them to the ranch where we had cages for such emergencies. They ate cottontails and jackrabbits immediately, so finding food for them was only a small problem.

Goswick and I returned to the capture site the following day and found the tracks of the mother lion. Within three hours, George's dogs had her in a tree. We redarted her, and took her to the ranch. During the time we had waited for her return, a new radio collar had arrived, and we felt that all was going as it should. We could reunite mother with kittens and release them all together—her with a signal-emitting collar that would allow us to follow their movements.

Our first sign of trouble came in our efforts to reunite young and mother. The adult was just beginning to recover from the drug when we placed the cubs in her cage. Her wobbly, abnormal behavior triggered something, and the young lions attacked. I'm not sure they could have killed her, being as small as they were, but they made every effort to do severe damage. We had to separate them.

This made our job much less certain. Our biggest concern had been that the mother would reject the kittens after all of the disturbance, and that she might kill them, thus our effort to reunite them while she was still drugged. Now we found ourselves in the situation of protecting the mother from the kittens. We placed their cage next to hers and let her recover. After she was fully awake, they all seemed to recognize each other and gave signs of wanting to be together. We placed one of the kittens in her cage, hoping it wasn't a sacrifice. She accepted it without a growl. We added the other two and all seemed well again.

The next morning, we hauled the family back to a point near the capture site and opened their cage. The female left the area at a trot; the kittens climbed nearby trees. We could only hope she would remember where she had left them.

Her radio signal over the next three days showed a steady drift southward, farther and farther from the capture site. Our only sighting of the kittens' tracks indicated that they had moved to the north—toward the capture site. Evidence suggested more strongly each day that the family was not reunited. Some ten days later, Goswick and Murphy found the nearly-starved kittens a short distance from the site of initial capture. Their dogs killed them on the ground before the hunters could intervene. The young were by this time too weak to climb trees.

The mother continued her southward drift for some ten days, then ceased moving in the middle of a large jumble of granite boulders. We hoped she had made a kill and intentionally left her alone for several days. When, after an additional week, she failed to move, we went in to check. We found her dead, curled up as if asleep, under a small alligator juniper. She, too, had apparently starved.

I should point out that we, and others, have handled mother lions with kittens more than once without such disastrous results. In this case, we probably should not have picked up the kittens in the first place. The mother would have ultimately returned for them. She must have been seeking a new kill in the interim. We never made the mistake of "saving" kittens again. Our compassion, in this case, is what killed them. The mother's death undoubtedly was due to inadequate food during the entire period of disruption. By the time she was back on her own, she was too weak to kill.

I'm not sure that all of the information we gained from this family group was worth the loss of lions, but we did learn. For one thing, we confirmed that the young go with the mother to kills fairly early in life and feed upon these kills. She undoubtedly leaves them at the kill site while she seeks new prey, and they apparently stay where they are left, regardless of disruptions.

Something I can't help but wonder at is the vulnerability of kittens at these kills. Although kills are normally buried, they still attract coyotes, ravens, vultures, and eagles. They probably also attract other adult lions. Kittens as small as the ones we observed (and we have seen several other under similar circumstances) certainly could be killed or injured by any of the above scavengers. Coyotes, eagles, and other mature lions could be especially damaging.

And yet kitten survival seems to be fairly high. In our studies, we saw no actual cases of natural mortality of small kittens. Maurice Hornocker, who pioneered mountain lion research in Idaho, documented the killing of a kitten by a mature male lion, and Ollie Barney, one of Arizona's better lion hunters, tells of finding an entire litter of three that had been killed at the site of a deer kill. He felt that the kittens and their mother were using a carcass that had been killed by an adult male lion. The male returned while the female was away and destroyed the kittens.

Some workers have suggested that adult males will not kill kittens that they have sired. Perhaps such a phenomenon exists in pride cats such as African lions. I don't think it has been proven to exist in the solitary cats, as yet.

The sign I've seen near kills used by kittens suggests that they do not spend all of their time in hiding. Kittens seem to have a glorious time at kills; and kill sites with kittens present take on a distinctive appearance—that of a minor tornado. Grass and ground litter may be disturbed for fifty feet surrounding such a carcass. Much rough and tumble romping apparently occurs. The body is usually more fully consumed than one used by a mature lion alone. Leg bones, ribs, and even the skull are chewed into small pieces. Chunks of hair, hide, ears, and tail are torn and scattered, suggesting that such fragments are used as toys. Nearby trees may have smaller limbs broken and will show claw marks where the juveniles have darted up and down their trunks. A kill with kittens present—judging by the sign—seems to be a busy place.

I'm not sure how long a female will leave kittens at kills before she returns. The female mentioned above stayed away six days, but this was after our presence, and our drugs, had disturbed her. How easily she makes another kill and how often she must return to eat undoubtedly have bearing. Prey density, thus, may affect the way a female behaves with relationship to kittens and kills, and this may influence kitten mortality. As prey density drops, a female may have to range farther and be gone longer to make kills. The longer her trips, the greater the likelihood of kitten losses. If killing of prey becomes too difficult, she may not return for the kittens, and they may be abandoned before they are old enough to survive.

The age at which kittens will survive without help from the mother is unknown, but limited evidence suggests that it may be less than six months. Bob Vaughn, an early lion hunter on the North Kaibab, told me of a hunt he made guiding Clark Gable. They treed and killed a female with a cub estimated at four months of age. The youngster was captured as an intended pet. They secured it to a tree with a chain and a spare dog collar, but the cub was gone the following morning. The chain remained, but the collar went with the lion.

A year later, the same lion, wearing the same and now very tight collar, was killed some thirty miles west of the point it had escaped. Vaughn, who had seen many lions in his lifetime, was convinced that the cub was no more than four months old when its mother was killed. How it managed to survive on its own is unknown, but it did survive. A male cub at this age will weigh no more than thirty to forty pounds.

Thirty years later, we captured two six- to seven-month-old lions not far from the spot where the Vaughn-Gable party killed their lion and captured their cub. These youngsters were independent of an adult and had killed a mature mule deer doe by themselves. They had done a relatively messy job of it. The ground surface was torn up around the kill location, much scratching and chewing was evident on the carcass of the deer. It died with considerable struggle—not the norm in lion-killed deer. The male cub of this pair weighed sixty-two pounds; the female fifty. We radio-collared these youngsters and documented the continued survival of the female (the male's collar failed within a week) for another five months. Sign indicated that the male was with her during this time, but we saw no evidence that they were ever accompanied by an adult. These kittens, too, were on their own at an early age. The female survived to adult-hood and produced at least one litter after crossing to the west side of the Kaibab.

Although refinement of technique certainly comes with expe-rience, killing of prey seems to be instinctive. Witness an instance involving captive-born two-year-old cougars that escaped from a zoo. These animals (four of them) killed seven goats and a vari-ety of smaller prey in a single night. Six-month-old captive cougars released under controlled conditions attacked and killed a mule deer fawn. Thus it seems that lion kittens are totally de-pendent through three to four months of age but have fair chances of survival alone after four to five months of age, given adequate prey densities.

CHAPTER THREE
Leaving Home and Settling Down

 The normal age for separating from the mother is about fourteen to twenty-four months. Whether this occurs through mutual consent of all concerned or via some devious behavior on the part of the adult is unknown. Some writers have suggested that it occurs as a result of rebreeding by the mother and that the presence of an adult male may aid in dispersing the young cats. Others feel that a simple tendency to drift apart occurs as the young become more proficient in survival. Recent evidence gathered on radioed lions seems to support the latter. The young seem first to dissociate from the mother, traveling together for a while. Then they, too, split. As in other aspects of lion behavior, however, much remains to be learned regarding the stages in gaining independence.

I find it curious that an animal starting in a litter becomes antisocial in adulthood. The earliest moments of a lion's life involve touching its siblings. Its growth involves play, interaction, and cooperation during early efforts at hunting. Yet the animal ultimately comes to avoid other adults except at breeding time.

Maurice Hornocker found young lions in Idaho dispersing from their areas of birth. He worked with a stable, socially-saturated lion population. He gave the term "transients" to these newly independent, subadult lions. Through the ages of approximately eighteen months to three years, they become mobile, homeless animals. As such, they constitute a particularly interesting age group, one that needs more study. In theory, they wander until they find an empty area to occupy, then settle for most of their life. Many questions remain to be answered regarding the mechanics of home area selection and the ultimate age when the selection is made.

Some evidence suggests that not all young lions leave their area of birth. If mortality of adult lions in the area of origin is high enough, the young, especially females, may simply occupy vacant territories near home. Exactly how a young lion determines the suitability of an area is unknown. Perhaps they move as a result of pressures from more dominant cats and cease to move when these pressures cease or when the transient lion becomes strong enough to displace an established adult. At least one researcher has suggested that the term transient should include both the young unestablished lions and the old, displaced adults. In Arizona's Superstition Mountains, we have radio-tracked one mature male that continued to drift over a six-year period. He used several areas temporarily but always moved on. Such a cat may be subdominant throughout its lifetime for some reason and be constantly displaced by superiors.

If these ideas are valid, the age at which young lions attain residency probably depends upon the density of the established lion population. As lion numbers increase, young lions take longer to find acceptable habitat. One wonders what happens to those young that fail to locate an available home area. Do they finally accept marginal habitat and ultimately die an early death? Or can lions actually exist at densities higher than studies to date would indicate? How does existing lion density affect their odds of survival? Studies in California, where the lion has been protected from hunting for almost sixteen years, may provide new insights into lion population dynamics.

Transient lions, especially the young ones, may be more troublesome to humans than established residents. A high percentage of recorded attacks on humans by lions seem to be made by this newly independent age group. Older, more established lions seem to have little inclination to attack people. I doubt that this is due to experience on the part of the older lions—they have little opportunity to encounter people, hence little chance for negative conditioning. I'm more inclined to believe that lions have an instinctive aversion to humans, but that hardship on the part of a young cat may drive it to attack people or pets.

Behavior of prey may also be important in determining the attack responses of a lion. They seem to react much like black bass to prey activity. A high proportion of recorded attacks on humans, for example, involved children at play. Propensity of lions to take calves and lambs, or to mass slaughter domestic sheep, may also be partially influenced by play or panic behavior of these animals, as opposed to the more sedentary behavior of other forms of domestic prey.

Whatever the case, young transients seem to get into trouble more often than other age classes, and this seems to stem from a conflict between their instinctive abilities to kill prey and their somewhat less well-developed ability to select appropriate prey. Two California workers noted that tame lions became more efficient at taking prey species after they had fed upon that particular prey. They seemingly needed to have items identified as food before they would actively hunt those particular items. Thus the prey they are taught to kill by their mother becomes important in their adult diet.

For transients, of course, eating is only one major problem. Finding a suitable home area is another. In general, the home areas of females, once established, seem to be more stable than those of males. I suspect that some bumping of old males by prime ones occurs. Females, conversely, seem to tolerate almost complete overlap of home areas, hence do not seem to displace each other. Gene sorting, via periodic territorial rearrangements, may thus be mainly the job of the male.

During our Spider Ranch studies, we observed apparent interactions of two mature males with adjoining ranges. One of these was a young prime lion in perfect condition. His home area encompassed some of the best lion habitat on the study area. The other was an old-timer, at least ten years in age. He ranged into country that was gentler, less brushy, and more populated by humans than that used by his neighbor. I suspect he had been gradually pushed out into this lesser habitat as he grew older. On two occasions, we found this old lion and the youngster in the same canyon at the same time, near the apparent boundary of their home areas. On both of these occasions, the old-timer moved out and was eight to ten miles away the next day. He seemingly was the subordinate animal of the pair. Young lions, especially males, may react to such pressures, continually moving until they find a spot where no pressures to move occur. This may explain why ranchers have experienced problems in trying to control lions. I'll discuss this in detail in a later section.

One area of controversy relates to fighting between males. Hornocker, in his Idaho study, found little sign of fighting. Workers in other states have suggested that considerable fighting between toms occurs and feel that they have seen physical evidence in the form of injuries and scars on male lions that they captured. Our Arizona studies disclosed no obvious evidence of fighting between males, but I've heard of such incidences from observers that I respect. One explanation is that fighting will be more common in a hunted lion population, where newly arrived lions are vying for the recently emptied home areas. This whole subject, however, is still open to conjecture.

Ultimately, at some point in their lives, most lions settle down. This probably occurs at about three to four years of age. Females may settle because of a successful breeding, or they may settle at an earlier age than males due to the apparent lack of need for exclusive home areas. Males may settle because they require more adequate space, and the behavior may be dependent upon mortality of other males in the population.

Once lions settle, they use a well-established home area for most of their lives. Males use larger areas than females, and as mentioned above, may be more inclined to rearrange their territories. The total area used by both sexes is determined by terrain, prey densities, and seasonal prey movements. In central Arizona, where no major seasonal shift of prey populations occurred, the lions used the same home areas year-round. On the Kaibab and in Idaho, where prey migrate between winter and summer ranges, lions adjust their movements, at least in part, to the seasonal movements of the prey.

Such long-term use of home areas has interesting genetic implications for the species. Because female home areas are smaller than those of males, several females may be overlapped by the area used by a single male. In an undisturbed lion population, the odds are high that a female will breed with the same male several times in her lifetime. Pairing occurs only during the heat period, so this mating is not enforced by any permanent pair bond. It occurs merely because of overlap of home areas. Nonetheless, sequential litters of a given female may very likely have the same father.

The isolation of lions from other lions during most of the year is so complete that one wonders how they manage to get together to breed. They are not limited to one season, so rutting, strutting, and ovulation are not synchronized as in deer or many birds. Lions do not, as far as we know, have breeding grounds or specific areas that serve to get the sexes together. Yet a species which socially enforces a low density of existence somehow joins males and females at the right time. Indications are that this is accomplished through a combined use of mobility and scent, although voice may also play a part. One old hunter has suggested that females in heat urinate on the scratches made by males, thus signaling readiness. Females in heat in zoos have been heard to yowl incessantly. I know of no one who has heard this sound in the wild, but I'm sure it occurs.

However it all happens, lions apparently breed within the home area of the female. The male drops by; the female doesn't go searching. From the limited evidence available, it appears that only one male is usually present. A male whose home area encompasses the home area of the female apparently does the job, hence the high odds of sequential breeding of the same male and female for several years. Dispersal of young transient animals is therefore essential to avoid inbreeding. If such dispersal is modified by the death of resident adults, whether naturally or through heavy kill by hunters (and this is as yet unknown), declining genetic health of the population could result. We need to know more about this phenomenon.

Breeding lions apparently stay together and move very little for several days. On two occasions, we have approached sedentary radioed females, expecting them to be on a kill, only to find them cohabiting with a male. I can envision, although I've not seen it, as much ruckus in lion breeding as occurs in house cats.

At least one male that I observed with a female showed signs of scratching, biting, and rough play in general. We assumed that the female had worked him over. His face, in particular, was covered with fine scratches. Such damage could be the source of some reports of male lions fighting.

Perhaps contradicting this scenario, we have a photograph, taken from an airplane, of a radioed female lying placidly under a juniper beside a larger unmarked lion, apparently a male, in a pose of complete domestic bliss. One Idaho researcher observed copulation between two wild lions, but I have not seen a published account of this occurrence. Nor have I seen detailed accounts of breeding in zoo animals.

Minimum breeding age is unknown. Some workers have speculated that a female will not breed until she has settled into a home area; others suggest that breeding stimulates settling. We have records on an adult female that was transplanted to a new area and bred while in an apparently unsettled state. She probably had bred earlier in her life, however, so may not represent the normal transient.

This particular cat was confiscated from trappers in Williams, Arizona. She had been captured some twenty miles northeast of that town. I held her in a cage at the Cross U Ranch until her foot healed, then released her about fifty miles southwest of her original site of capture. Approximately one year later, she turned up on a calf kill twenty-five miles southwest of the release site. She was accompanied by a four-month-old kitten.

The lion had bred during the period of unsettledness. The calf she killed was in an open prairie, several miles from anything resembling good lion habitat. Being settled in an area is therefore apparently not absolutely essential to breeding; perhaps breeding is a prerequisite to settling. In highly saturated lion populations, I suspect that young females breed and lose litters because they are forced to exist in submarginal habitats.

As an aside, the only other lion we have transplanted in Arizona followed a movement pattern similar to that of the above female. This was a mature male that had been trapped on a deer kill near lower Beaver Creek. We released him after he had healed about twenty-five airline miles northwest of his original capture site. He turned up four years later some seventy-five miles west of the release site. He had killed seven domestic sheep and was trapped by a federal control agent. Transplanted lions do not seem to stay put or stay out of trouble.

Under natural conditions, however, lions, or at least female lions, seem to be extremely tenacious within their range. Our first lion marked on the Spider Ranch was a mature female of at least three years of age when initially captured in November 1971. We radio-tracked her and recaptured her periodically through the spring of 1976. She stayed within the same fifty-odd square miles during this entire period and produced three litters. She was finally killed by hunters during the spring of 1981, still well within the known area of use. Males may be equally tenacious, although, as mentioned, limited evidence suggests that they can be displaced by prime males as they grow older. Such older displaced males may once again become a part of the transient lion population. This could explain the periodic catch of old lions in areas that are heavily hunted.

Daily movements of lions within their home areas have long been a subject of speculation with hunters. One of the most common myths holds that lions make regular circuits and that, once the circuit is discovered, the interval at which a lion passes given points can be predicted. Around every seven to eight days seems to be a common figure. None of this matches known fact. Radioed lions monitored in various locations have not followed such regular routes. They seem to move freely within their home areas. They make use of major drainages, rims, and saddles because these offer the easiest passage through the country, but they do not necessarily pass these topographic features at regular intervals. Common sense, in fact, would rule against such regularity, for it would require regularity in making kills, eating, and other aspects of lion behavior. Such routine is probably more a characteristic of humans than of wildlife. It is true that lions have favorite bedding sites within their home areas and can be found lying up in certain spots with fair frequency. Even here, however, regularity cannot be expected.

In trailing lions with dogs, one gets the feeling that the cats have two basic movement modes: hunting and traveling. If you fall on the track of a lion looking for prey, you will spend your day rambling through a limited area on a crooked path. The dogs wlll overrun the track frequently, and movement will be slow. You may trail all day and never get more than two or three airline miles from your starting point. If you jump the lion, it may be on a fresh kill and have a full stomach. Your chase to the tree will be short.

A traveling cat, however, is a different situation, especially if it's a male. Lions changing places will take fairly direct routes and will cover many miles. Even though your dogs may trail such a straight track more rapidly, you may go all day on such a track and end up far from camp. You may also never jump the lion.

To this point, I've written mainly about the biology of the lion—its birth and progress to adulthood. If the lion were the only component in the concept of cougar, we could wrap up the book with a few more biological details. The lion, while perhaps physically difficult to study, is actually a relatively simple beast in its lifestyle. But its lifestyle conflicts with some human lifestyles, and this in turn creates conflict in the human population as a whole, for not everyone agrees on how to deal with the lion. In fact, the lion, along with a few other large carnivores, has become a symbol of the contentiousness that surrounds dwindling wildlands and wild species on our planet. Few symbols will more rapidly disclose the basic philosophical differences in people.

So let us turn for a while to the human elements in the concept of cougar.

SECTION TWO

THE
HUMAN
ELEMENT

CHAPTER FOUR
The Array

 Two widely separated viewpoints exist regarding the purpose of the planet earth. At one extreme are those who would domesticate the world, making it controlled and productive for our species. Insatiable land developers fit within this role. Extremists in the rancher or hunter camp may also approach this point of view. To them, nothing in creation has a value of its own except as it serves humankind. At the other end of the spectrum are the preservationists, who seem to value all of nature *except* humankind. Obviously, these extremes skirmish constantly over symbols such as the cougar. If we can believe Eric Hoffer in his book, *The True Believer*, however, extremists are extremists regardless of their point of view. The common element is their need to believe. Both sides seem to seek final solutions. The interesting part of all of this is that you can occasionally catch them outside of their beliefs and discover them to be real human beings.

I remember a spring day on Spider Ranch. Mid-afternoon temperatures were nudging eighty degrees. It was already too hot for lion hunting. Soil on open south slopes held little scent. Odds were not good, but we were hunting lions and we had a track.

We also had a guest—a representative of one of the more influential animal defense groups in the country. He was, you might say, investigating our operation. His group had helped fund our project but had doubts about its value and was uneasy about the harrassment and handling to which we subjected the cats. Many of the people behind him felt that wildlife research would be unnecessary if the animals were simply protected from all human intervention.

A second guest had arrived unexpectedly with the protectionist. We caught him a horse and brought him along. I was surprised to learn, as the day progressed, that he had no particular drum to beat. He was present for the adventure. Unlike his partner, he admitted to enjoying deer hunting and upland bird shooting. He had, in fact, considered hiring a guide to bag a lion, but it was not something he felt pressed to do. His friendship with the preservationist, it seemed, centered around other interests.

We were in the third year of the lion study. Our job was to tree, dart, mark, and radio-track lions, with a view to finding out how many lived in this particular chunk of country and how much beef and venison they were eating. At this point in my relationship with lions, I really didn't know how I felt about them. I was, at least, unable to relate strongly to either the rigid economic standards of the cowboy or the moralistic viewpoint of the preservationist. I was perhaps more concerned than the average sportsman only because my job placed a certain amount of responsibility for management decisions regarding lions upon my shoulders. We were all of about the same generation. The cowboy-guide and I were perhaps four or five years older than our guests, but we were all between thirty-five and forty-five—basically products of the era of rapid technological advances of the forties, fifties, and sixties. Yet each of us was on the hunt for a different reason. Our feelings varied greatly in intensity. Our basic differences were essentially absolute, as if we belonged to different species.

Our regular hunter, George Goswick, was busy at his ranch, so I approached a local ranch foreman known to be a capable lion hunter for help. If he accepted the invitation, this would be the first time in his life that our cowboy-guide had been placed in direct contact with "one of them damned environmentalists." When I had approached him about the hunt a week or so earlier, he had recoiled at the idea. He wanted nothing to do with "the meddling bastard." After giving the matter some thought, however, a twinkle had come to his eye, and he reckoned he might "teach the sonofabitch a thing or two about lions and wear his fat ass out in the process."

As it turned out, "fat ass" was not an apt description for the protectionist. He and the guide were equally lean, hard, and sunburned: the guide from long hours in the saddle and an active outdoor job, the city man from wilderness hikes and, probably, jogging the streets when he was not in the woods. Looking at them, I was ashamed of my bureaucrat's belly, formed as a result of too many hours of paper-shuffling and too many beers used in place of jogging to relieve tensions. I, too, spent long hours in the woods but never seemed to attain the condition of these two men who were so totally devoted to their chosen lifestyles. Perhaps looseness of mind produces looseness of belly. The fourth member of the party, the guest, was pretty much average in build, demeanor, and, as far as I could tell, condition.

The hunt was not easy. While our stopping point at the end of the day was no more than two airline miles from our starting point, we covered perhaps seven or eight miles on the ground due to the wandering route the lion followed. We traveled slowly, taking seven hours to cover this distance; the heat made tracking difficult for the dogs. Just sitting in the saddle can be tiring for those unaccustomed to riding. The preservationist commented two or three times that he wondered why we bothered with horses. He could keep up easily on foot and was actually off his horse more than on, trusting his own feet in steep terrain over those of the quadruped.

Our guide was afoot much of the time, too, but for a different reason. He had to help the dogs frequently where the track had burnt out. The dogs followed only their noses. When the scent became too faint, they lost the track. The sharp eye of the guide supplemented the noses of the hounds. He regularly pushed his way through the thickets of turbinella oak and manzanita to search for some obscure mark that only he could identify as a lion track. Once the track was relocated, the dogs were called and started again, only to bog down once more on the next southerly exposure.

I helped where I could, but was only beginning to develop the skill of finding tracks on the dry, rocky slopes. I had almost messed up earlier in the day, right after the dogs had opened. We knew they were on a lion, but we weren't sure they were trailing in the right direction. I noticed a lion scratch made by a cat

---

29

heading the opposite way from the dogs and immediately started calling to turn them around. The guide checked my scratch and disdainfully said he felt the dogs were on something fresher. He rapidly turned the dogs back in their original direction. I was grumpily thinking that he just didn't want me to show him up in front of the guests, when he called me. In the sandy bottom of a wash was the fresh track of a very large tom, undoubtedly made some time during the preceding night. The dogs and the guide were on the right end.

I refrained from helping for a good part of the morning until the guide, perhaps sensing my embarrassment, started asking me to "check that draw over there and see if you can see the track." As the day wore on, tracking grew more difficult for the dogs. With each hour, the scent faded. Our guide scrambled over granite boulder piles and climbed steep slopes of rotten granite to find the track and move the dogs another quarter mile. The protectionist marveled at the ability of the guide to negotiate the rough country in his leather-soled cowboy boots. Both of our guests wore the best in padded hiking boots with Vibram soles. The guide had warned them early in the day about not putting such boots too deep in the stirrups.

The younger dogs began to give up and sought the shade of junipers. Water was scarce, and when we found a shallow pot-hole in a wash bottom, the dogs lay in it and drank it dry. Only the two oldest dogs and the guide persisted on the track.

Conversation through most of the day stayed stilted and almost formally polite. The guide, determined to make his point, had told several tales of "poor little calves" killed by lions. I grinned inwardly at these remarks, because I had helped him butcher a yearling for our own consumption only two weeks before. The protectionist remained quiet through this, then asked a few pointed questions regarding the rights of ranchers on public lands. The guide let it be known that "publicness" of lands was subject to interpretation and that he felt that a certain amount of control of the lands went along with the grazing permits. With boundaries thus established, the guide gave full attention to directing the hunt, the preservationist to observing.

I began to sense that our guests, both of them, were as keen as we on catching a lion. The preservationist demonstrated his disappointment and impatience every time the dogs lost the track. His excitement paralleled that of the dogs when the scent freshened on cool slopes. His sportsman friend gently kidded him for letting his "hunting blood" get up.

I began to have serious doubts about catching the cat. The hunt was developing like many I'd seen before. You trail until three or four in the afternoon, the dogs give out, the scent fades, and you gather the pack and go home. Tomorrow, you look for another, fresher track. This was the pattern three out of four times. There were days when you wondered if you really had ever caught a lion.

About this time, the dogs trailed off into an extremely rough canyon some five hundred feet deep. Both walls of the canyon were strewn with large basalt boulders and heavy thickets of oak, garrya, manzanita, cat claw, and ceanothus. A horse could not cross the canyon at this point, and it was a long, half-hour loop around its head.

The track was fresher on the shaded side of the canyon; the dogs literally charged to the bottom and a quarter of the way up the far side. Beyond this canyon, I knew from previous hunts, lay a broad open plateau with sparse juniper and dry, sandy soil. It would not hold scent. If the lion track led us there, we would be finished for the day. The sun was already low, and we had perhaps an hour and a half of daylight left at best. If we went much further, we'd be handling the lion and riding out after dark. I'd done this before and didn't enjoy it. With novice riders, it would be even less fun.

The dogs still hadn't moved from the opposite slope of the canyon. They seemed totally confused. Twenty minutes passed and they continued to mill, returning to our side of the canyon, then trailing across to the other. I was about to suggest that we call them in and head home when we spotted motion in the brush fifty feet below the milling dogs.

At first, because of its color, I thought it was one of the red-bone hounds in the pack, but a single eight-foot leap across a chasm between two boulders showed me my error. The cat had been found. The brush was so high and thick that the dogs couldn't see the lion, but they knew he was close. He moved a short distance, then crawled into a cave under a rock. A pup blundered into him, backed up three steps, and started a frenzied baying. The cat slipped around the rock, evaded the pup, and hid again before the pack could surround him.

The massive granite boulders formed a near-vertical maze. We could see into it from our vantage point, but the dogs could only move laboriously through it. The lion moved both through it, and by spanning boulders, across it. He hid, moved, and hid again, working slowly upward toward the opposite rim of the canyon. The boulders provided him a myriad of escape routes above the heads of the dogs.

Excitement increased within our group. The guide encouraged the dogs with loud whistles and "sic-ums." He slapped his knee and laughed when the lion jumped clean over a bewildered pup. "That'll make him a lion dog!" Once, in a lull, he commented, "If that cat gets over that rim, we'll probably lose him. Those dogs are about burnt out."

As the lion approached the top, I tensed. The guide was right. The cat would probably leave the dogs if he hit the sandy flat on the far side, or if they stayed with him, they might be out of hearing by the time we headed the canyon. Most certainly it would be dark.

My concentration on the lion was so complete that I forgot other members of the party and their various affiliations. The sportsman-observer, however, remained a bit more detached. He had stayed to the rear and observed the scene with a bit of calm humor. As the lion approached the point of seeming escape, the sportsman eased alongside me on his horse and lightly tapped my arm. He had a delightful twinkle in his eye as he quietly directed my attention to the protectionist and the guide who were standing side by side on a large rock, both hollering loudly at the dogs, "Get him! Get the sonafabitch! Get him!"

The day ended with a newly marked lion, and we reached our vehicles before dark, feeling our efforts had yielded success. The purpose of these efforts, of course, was to gather data on lions, but, as had happened on this day, involvement in the study put me in contact with proponents of all of the various viewpoints regarding the lion. I found my stereotypes of these groups breaking down, and as a relatively neutral observer, I found elements in all of them that I could value, even if my feelings didn't run as strong as theirs. Each of them became a portion of my concept of cougar. Starting with hunters, I'd like to look at them one by one.

CHAPTER FIVE
Hunters and Hounds

One can hunt lions in several ways. Only one really works: using good dogs. A few lions are killed each year by people hunting other wildlife species. Lions have been killed by rabbit hunters using .22 rimfire rifles. Quail hunters have killed lions at short range using shotguns with light birdshot. In Arizona, the mass influx of deer hunters into the woods each fall results in the death of several lions. Such opportunistic hunters cannot be considered lion hunters per se. They just happened to have been in the right place to shoot a lion and had the desire to do so. In the vast expanses of the West, such instances are relatively rare and, alone, have little impact on total lion numbers. In the East, more uniform distribution of humans may have been a major factor in the cougar's extinction there.

People who attract lions with predator calls also fit into the opportunist category. They are usually calling coyotes, bobcats, or fox—species that are abundant enough to be consistently within hearing of calls. A few callers have learned to focus their efforts on the places where lions lie up, thus increasing the odds of bringing in a big cat. At least one Arizona hunter has called twelve lions over a period of ten years or so. As far as I know, this is a record. When you compare this with lifetime records of dog men such as the Goswick or the Lees, who have perhaps accounted for over a thousand lions each, calling seems ineffective.

Lion hunting, therefore, is hunting with hounds. Those who have trained a good pack of dogs and consistently catch lions consider lion hunting the king of sports on our continent. I'm inclined to agree, and I don't kill lions. Unfortunately, the current popular view of lion hunting with hounds, as displayed by television, shows a pack of wild-running, untrained dogs released on an already-jumped lion. These are followed by hunters in helicopters or jeeps until the cat is run into the ground and killed.

It seems to acknowledge little skill on the part of the hunter. In fairness to lion hunters, an overview of what lion hunting really entails is appropriate here.

Probably no sport requires more investment of time than hunting with hounds, regardless of the wildlife species pursued. A well-trained bird dog, for example, can be hunted a few days each fall and still perform as a bird dog. True, top gun dogs aren't made with such a casual approach, but the instincts of bird dog breeds are strong. If your standards aren't extremely high, you can have a bird dog that appears to be a bird dog with little reinforcement between hunting seasons.

Such is not the case with hounds. For one thing, except in a few southeastern states where deer are hunted with dogs, the species most people pursue with hounds are not among the true natural prey of the canids. Hounds, like all dogs, are basically predators. As anyone who has gone afield with a half-grown pup can tell you, hounds will by instinct trail prey species such as deer and rabbits. They may react to the warm scent of any animal, but they instinctively follow things that smell like food.

The trick in training hounds lies in getting them to trail only the species you want to catch. With lion hounds, this is especially difficult. There are far more deer and rabbits, or even coyotes and bobcats, in lion country than there are lions. In most of the West, there are also more bears, at least in summer and fall. As a result, simply getting a pack of untrained dogs through a maze of stronger, more abundant, and more attractive scents and ultimately to a treed lion seems almost impossible. Few untrained dogs will trail a lion on first exposure to scent, even in fresh snow. The rare one that does will usually stay with it only as far as the first fresh deer track.

Few people have experienced the feeling of rage, frustration, and total helplessness that comes from trying to control a pack of trashy, untrained hounds. A neophyte goes afield with the hope that maybe, just maybe, things will click and the day will end with a big cat in a tree. With a fresh snow just six inches deep and a day off in the middle of the week, things could not be better. Weekend hunters won't be running the roads, so the hunt shouldn't turn into a four-wheel-drive backroad rally.

The dogs are still an unknown quantity: they are all young and inexperienced. But that blue pup did tree the neighbor's cat out back the other day. He even bawled on its track once before he jumped it out of the hedge. Everyone says that if a dog will tree housecats, it will tree lions. Maybe today is the day.

And you find a track early—crisp in the fresh snow. No doubt about its being a lion. Nothing else that big with pad and toes could be out here. The three lobes in the heel are diagnostic. You release the dogs and the blue pup bawls instantly on the track. The other pups bawl just for the hell of it and take off at a run—ninety degrees from the lion's direction of travel. Within a half mile, you hear a high-pitched squeal from one of the pups that says something, probably a deer is jumped. Then comes the cacophony of the whole pack in chase. You shout obscenities until you're hoarse, trying to catch a lull in the dogs' barking so that they might hear you. But you know it's no use.

You go back to the car and wait. The blue pup, of course, went with the rest of them as soon as the chase became exciting. Shortly, the youngest dog starts wailing lost at the bottom of the nearest deep canyon and won't come when you call him. You climb into the steep gorge, pull the pup, at the peril of your own life, off of the ledge where he bluffed up and lead (actually drag) him back to your vehicle. Out of exasperation, you stick his nose in the lion track, but he's already beat for the day and merely hunches guiltily at your feet. You suppress an urge to kick him, knowing he'd undoubtedly connect the punishment with the smell of the lion track. He cocks an ear at the distant sound of bawling dogs, and you decide you'd better put him in a box before he breaks again and goes with the others.

You drive roads the remainder of the day, hoping to pick up dogs, but none come out. You leave a little food and your best hunting coat under a bush near the spot where you originally parked, hoping the dogs will stay put if they do come in. For the next two evenings, you drive the roads after work and slowly pick up a dog here and another there. Your hunting coat disappears the second night, with no tracks to indicate who might have taken it. One evening, you have to work late and your wife makes the run for you (hunting is a family sport). She hasn't returned by the time you get off, so you borrow a friend's four-wheeler and finally find her at midnight, stuck and cranky at the end of a two-rut trail. By the end of the week you have only one dog out, but it is the blue pup who holds so much promise. He's the best, so naturally he'd stay longer.

After another week of worrying and driving roads, you get a call from a nice old lady in a village near your hunting ground. She tells you the dog wandered into her place the evening of the same day you lost him. She just hadn't noticed your name tag on his collar until that morning. She wishes you'd come and get him, though, because he keeps eating all the food she puts out for her cat, and the cat hasn't been out from under the house for nine days.

That, in a nutshell, is a beginner's approach to lion hunting and a stage that most of us have gone through to some degree or other. Many who try to hunt lions never pass this stage. They either eventually give up in despair after a year or two of dog roundups, or they spend the rest of their lives with two or three overfed hounds staked in the back yard and tell lion-hunting tales to anyone who will listen. They speak vaguely of lions caught, but you can never pin them down to numbers. Such hunters do little damage to lion populations, but they may damage severely the image of the sport.

To advance beyond this stage requires determination, will at least stronger than that of the hounds, possibly expenditure of a goodly sum of money, and quite a bit of luck. The first step to success is to begin hunting with an experienced and successful hunter who has good, trained dogs. The next step is to lay out dollars for a well-started dog of your own. You have to have a hound that will follow a lion track and will stay with it regardless of other scents it may cross. In spite of all the advertisements in hound magazines, such dogs are hard to find. You can spend a fortune shipping dogs back and forth on trial and still have nothing useful. If and when you do find a started dog, you can expect to pay at least $500 to $1000 for him. You can expect to pay twice that for an old, well-broke dog. With a started dog, you can begin to train pups, one or two at a time. If you have the perseverence, time, and money, you will in a matter of years begin to catch lions with fair regularity.

A good lion dog, of course, is a dog that will catch lions. I have never seen a set of standards for the ideal lion hound. Coon hunters, with their water races and night chases, have developed a complex set of standards concerning the ideal cooner. I'm not well acquainted with their forms of competition, so can't evaluate the usefulness of their standards in judging lion dogs.

In essence, when one talks of lion dogs, he talks of a pack and must almost assess dogs at the pack level rather than on the basis of individuals. This is not to say that one dog alone can't catch lions. It happens. A pack of four to eight dogs working well together, however, will tree many more cats than even the best single hound will ever catch. In addition, a hunter must be looking ahead and developing new dogs; for a serious hunter, hunting a single dog does not make sense.

The ideal dog is one that will search ahead of the hunter for a track, will bawl when it finds the track, and will not bawl on other species. Once on a track, the ideal hound will continue to work the scent in one direction as long as it can extract scent. When a lion is jumped, the dog will pursue it by sight or scent until it is pushed to tree, rock, or cave.

While many dogs will chase and tree game once it is jumped, few will learn to open on a single species and work the track for the long hours needed to locate lions. A lion dog trails the lion where it walked the night before, or at times, two or three nights before. A good dog can detect scent on cool, dry slopes as many as three or four days after the tracks were made. They may not be able to trail such old scent for extended periods, but they will find spots where it can still be smelled.

I might interject here that the lion hunter is also part of the pack. He is the brains (although I've heard it questioned whether lion hunters have brains) and must give guidance to the pack. The hunter must retain control.

Few lion dogs, for instance, can tell the direction of movement of a lion from scent alone. Coon dogs, bear dogs, and bloodhounds trailing humans apparently seldom err in track direction. For some reason, the fore and aft of a lion track is more difficult to ascertain. Perhaps it is the roundness of the track, hence relatively undifferentiated distribution of the scent. Whatever the cause, a dog will usually follow a lion track in the direction the dog is moving when it finds the track. I have owned only one dog that I suspected to be able to detect direction of travel of a lion, at least part of the time. I was never totally certain about him.

I once hunted for a day with a newcomer to the sport who claimed that his dogs would not follow a backtrack. He had paid big money for the pack and had good dogs. They struck a fairly warm track early in the day, and I began to cast around to see it. The hunter informed me in stern terms that his dogs needed no help, so I left the hunting to him. Within a half mile, however, I saw the track clearly in the dust, headed the way we had just come. I was fully offended by this time and spitefully refused to inform the hunter of his dogs' error. We backtracked for six hours that day, and I declined to go afield with the hunter the next.

A hunter's first responsibility, then, is to determine the direction of travel of the cat. On snow, this is not a problem; on hard, dry ground, one can spend hours trailing in the wrong direction before crossing a visible track. The success of a hunt can depend upon the simple chance of hitting the track right in the first place. Actually seeing a track is usually the only sure way to know its direction. If a male lion is the quarry, scratches may tell which way he has gone. Females rarely, if ever, make scratches.

Once the dogs are lined out on a track, if it is a fresh one and if the dogs are reliable, the hunter can relax and just tag along. A good trail horse or mule adds immensely to the ease and pleasure of the hunt. If the track is a tough one, and most of them are, the hunter may spend more time off the horse searching for tracks than riding. Part of the art of hunting is knowing when to help the dogs and when to let them keep working a track on their own. Taking over too quickly can make the dogs dependent on the hunter. It can also confuse them and cause them to reverse direction or pull off entirely.

When working a difficult track, having several good dogs helps. On dry ground, trailing is a matter of scenting in one spot, then searching ahead until the scent is found again. It is not a process of smelling systematically from track to track. Dogs will catch a bit of scent on the ground, rocks, or brush, then dash ahead twenty to thirty yards before they smell again. If they dash in the wrong direction, at an angle to the actual direction of the track, they will have to relocate the line of the track. If the lion has made a turn, the dogs may dash far off-line between scents and may lose considerable time in relocating. Trailing is not done just on the ground. Body scent attaches to brush, and a track may be worked much faster in thick brush than on bare ground.

The idea, of course, is to trail the lion where it walked the night before and stay on the trail until the cat is jumped. Lions normally bed up in thick brush or boulders or under overhanging ledges in midday. As a result, daytime tracking, if you are on the right end of the track, and if the track itself isn't too long, should lead you to the lion. You hope for the right end and short end of the track. If you start at or near the point the lion started the previous night, the dogs simply may not be able to trail fast enough to catch up during a single day. Many lion hunts consist of following the trailing dogs through rough country from daylight to dark without catching the cat.

Old-time hunters, such as Ben Lilly, reputedly solved this problem by gathering dogs and sleeping where the night found them, then going on the next day or the next until the cat was caught. I personally have my doubts about how often such hunts really happened. In my limited experience, a full day of hard tracking can do in a pack of dogs. Two full days will often totally dampen their enthusiasm. I suspect that many of these supposed three- or four-day hunts were really a matter of the hunter camping in the country a given lion was using and cutting sign until he hit the short end of a night-old track. This approach would probably be more productive than continuous trailing.

In most areas, the home ranges of mature male lions run one hundred to one hundred fifty square miles; mature females range over twenty-five to fifty square miles. These figures vary with terrain, prey density, and other factors, but they are close to the average. One hundred and fifty square miles sounds like a lot of territory, but it really amounts to an area some twelve to thirteen miles on the side. Except in rare instances where a hunter is trailing a transient lion or in situations where lions may range between insular mountain ranges, extended tracks going over eight to ten miles are unlikely. A hunter working a slow, cold track is probably better off to pull his dogs and circle ahead rather than slowly pound the track. Being able to judge when and where to pull dogs is an important part of successful lion hunting.

All of the above, of course, becomes moot if you do not have good lion hounds. Unless you can afford good dogs from the beginning, developing an adequate pack may be the most difficult job of all. Hounds, in fact all hunting dogs, are merely an extension of the man, and the man an extension of the hounds. Their relationship is cooperative, but make no mistake, the man must be dominant. Uncontrolled hounds are simply wild, running predators. They seek prey at random.

Herein lies the trick to training hounds. You do not train them to do something—to retrieve, to sit, lie down, and so on. You train to eliminate undesirable behavior while retaining the desirable. The breeding of hounds over the years has focused on hunting—principally trailing and treeing abilities. By nature, predators hunt prey species such as deer, rabbits, and rodents. In the natural state, it would have been inefficient, I think, for hound ancestors to pursue other predators or even prey species that went to tree. A treeing predator in nature would have starved to death at the base of the tree, and with his barking, would have brought every other predator in the country to observe his demise (or contribute to it).

Thus the propensity to trail and tree must be an offshoot of play behavior that has been capitalized upon by dog breeders through the generations. Until a few months ago, I was convinced that it really had no parallel in nature. However, Todd

Soderquist of the Arizona Game and Fish Department sent me a note describing an incident where a lion was actually trailed and bayed by a pair of coyotes. It was a short-lived observation and seemed to involve play behavior. So here is at least one solidly-documented instance of coyotes acting something like hounds. I've since heard of a similar incident observed by a cowboy on the Mogollon Rim.

Such trailing of a predator could, I suppose, have practical advantages in nature. David Mech, who has spent a lifetime working with wolves, believes that they do not bark or howl on the trail of prey. Sounding on the track would, it seems, be disadvantageous to a single predator, for it would forewarn the prey. Mech notes that wolves have barked at him when he had driven them from a kill. Treeing could be a derivative of this type of behavior. One cannot help but wonder if wolves ever treed lions at kills.

In fact, it is possible that trailing, sounding, and treeing are an extremely specialized form of behavior that actually functioned in the wild state. While barking on the track of prey species would have been counterproductive, barking on the track of other predators might make sense. If a canid could learn that, by trailing a large cat, he could find fresh meat, he would have cause to call for help. Communal treeing at a kill would allow all involved eventually to feed.

Trailing and scent are little understood by humans. We do not live by our noses, hence we know little about the subtleties of smells. I read, in the tracking dog literature, of ground scent and air scent. My observations in working hounds make me wonder about the existence of a residual air scent. I cannot believe it would last more than a moment without disruption by breezes. Scent carried by air is a reality. Dogs can scent animals if they stand downwind from them. I suspect, however, that most trailing, even after animals are jumped, is done using ground or body scent on brush.

We talk of the need for ground moisture to trail. Perhaps what we're really wanting is a sign of the freshness of the track. Hounds generally move a fresh track in snow quite easily. If a snow track is melted out by the sun, then freezes, it can be quite difficult for dogs to smell. If it again thaws slightly, it will have more scent. Scent can be frozen into a track.

A track on wet ground can be trailed easily when it is fresh. However, the scent will disappear from the moist surface faster than from surrounding dry surfaces. Evaporation of the moisture carries the scent away with it. Cold-nosed dogs on an old track will invariably take their scents from cool dry rocks or brush. Both of these hold scent longer than a moist, but drying, soil surface.

Pine needles, dust, or other surfaces consisting of loose debris will not hold scent well. Experienced dogs work around such surfaces and look for better places to trail. Scent from a track can become faint in midday heat, then become fresher again as the ground cools in the evening. Thus a track lost in midday might be resumed successfully in early evening.

Many methods have been devised to break hounds from trailing the wrong game (called trash by houndsmen). Some hounds break easily; others never quite get over chasing deer or coyotes. Severe punishment seldom makes much difference. Some of the best dogs I've seen have been in the hands of those houndsmen that seemed to punish the least but do it at the right times. Showing hounds the desired game—positive reinforcement—seems to work best of all in training.

Nonetheless, the hound advertisements abound with solutions and scents of unwanted game to be used in negative conditioning of trashy dogs, and many exotic techniques for applying these scents have been developed. A common tool is to cage an errant canine with deer scent, or even deer parts, in a barrel rigged much like those once used for lottery drawings, and crank away. The wild ride associated with the scent is supposed to do the trick. I've also heard of injecting a nausea-inducing drug, then releasing a dog on a trash trail. Collars designed to shock the dog during the unwanted act are one of the best modern tools for training particularly stubborn hounds. They rapidly get the dogs' full attention, and they damage only their pride.

Actually the truth of hound training, assuming a modicum of

hunting with the dogs to provide positive experience, is that some dogs have it and some dogs don't. Each hound is different, and the hunter ultimately must adjust his technique to the pack he has working at any particular time. We developed our own pack while hunting with professional hunters on Spider Ranch and later used this pack to catch our own lions on the North Kaibab. In so doing, we tried perhaps sixty hounds, ending with only four that were good enough to be memorable.

We had several that were memorable for other reasons. We tried Joshua, for instance, a top-line registered black and tan who ultimately came to be known for his booming voice (used only when chasing deer and disrupting the pack), his earspread (twenty-eight inches tip to tip, undoubtedly a Boone and Crockett record for dogs), and his ability to sleep soundly under a treed lion in the midst of any number of wildly baying hounds.

And there was Scooter, a bluetick of unknown breeding, whose favorite game was porcupines. On the Spider Ranch, where we failed to see a porcupine during five years of intensive field work, Scooter almost weekly appeared with his face full of quills. He was drugged more than any lion on the area, for we soon learned that putting him to sleep was the easiest way to relieve him of his prickly burdens. He may have become a drug addict.

The stories of hounds that we knew, good and bad, would make another book. Perhaps it will. For our present purposes, though, the best approach is to follow a pack of experienced hounds through a hunt the way it really happened. This will demonstrate better than any other way the nuances of hunting lions with hounds and may show why dogs are also a major element in the concept of cougar.

CHAPTER SIX
A Classic Hunt

I can't say that this is an average lion hunt. I don't know what average is. It combined nearly all of the events possible. It is the kind of hunt I would choose to give anyone who wants to see dogs and hunters work, and it comes close in my mind to being perfect. It is told as it happened.

I feel a need to make a bit of a disclaimer before continuing the story. Norm Woolsey and I are the principals in this hunt. It happened toward the end of the five years we spent capturing and marking lions on the Spider Ranch, aided by such worthies as George Goswick, Bill Workman, Ollie Barney, Clell Lee, and Dale Lee. These men were our teachers, and I don't want to steal their thunder by excluding them here. However, it is easier to describe the fine details of a hunt where Norm and I were doing all of the work. If any of the above hunters read this, I hope they take pride in their professorship.

We were able to start the track early, because we had a known kill. We had checked the mule deer carcass for the past two mornings, hoping that the cat would return. It hadn't. We knew it was a male, a large one, from the size of the track. Our hope was waning, but we had crawled from our beds at four and driven one more time to the Camp Wood vicinity. This time it worked.

The ground was bare, without snow, but it held moisture. You could scrape the surface with your toe and see dampness below. This gave ideal conditions for scent retention. The dry surface held the scent, the moisture below helped keep the ground cool. A wetter surface would probably lose scent as it dried. We had parked our vehicle at the sign that said "Cottonwood Cabin–7 Miles," in sight of the old Paddocks Ranch. Paddocks was an idyllic spot with two cabins and fenced pasture that had been annexed by the Spider-Cross U Ranch complex. It no longer stood as a separate ranch but served as a summer cabin or lodging for temporary help for the Cross U.

Norm Woolsey, my companion, had grown up on the Arizona-New Mexico border near Safford and Silver City. He had hunted and trapped the mountains of Arizona his entire life. His experience with hounds was limited when he came to the lion study (as was mine), but his broad outdoor experience and interest in predators made him a natural for the project. Working hounds came easily to him. Norm seldom tried to impress anyone. He disclosed his skills and knowledge only as situations demanded.

It was just daylight when we rode away from the vehicle. With us, we had Chink, my red strike dog, and Rattler, a four-year-old Walker-redtick mix who could move a track as fast as any dog I've seen but who could never quite get over chasing deer if there was no lion track to work. Rattler bored easily, and although I learned to identify a particular twinkle in his eyes that appeared on mornings he had deer-chasing in mind, I was never able to stop his trashing completely. Moonshine was also along. He was a two-year-old Walker-bluetick mix who had just started to work well on lions. Our remaining working dog was Norm's black and tan bitch, Bonnie. She was a bit hyper to my way of thinking (the other guy's dogs always have faults) but would pound a lion track all day and tree hard. In addition to this base pack, we had two young dogs on trial. These were Walker-mix dogs given to us by Bill Workman of Tonto Basin. They were unknowns. We definitely had more dogs than we needed, but by necking the young ones together, we maintained a semblance of control. In necking dogs, you use a short strap or rope about eight inches long with snaps on each end. These snaps are simply hooked to the collar rings of a pair of dogs so that they are forced to travel in unison (theoretically). This doesn't totally prevent them from chasing trash, but it usually makes trash-chasers easier to intercept and punish. Necked dogs will usually learn to stay close after a few tries at running away.

Chink told of the lion's presence before we reached the site. I knew he was smelling lion scent before he opened. The rate with which his tail wagged and the intensity with which he sucked scent from the ground both increased until he could no longer restrain the sharp chopping barks that were building in his throat. The tone of the bark told us lion had been present and that the smell was strong.

I dismounted and began to look for a visible track. Rattler and Moonshine erupted into a wailing plea to be released from their necking chains. They, too, knew that Chink was straight. I would not release them, however, until I knew that we were following the track in the right direction. Tracks around kills, where the lion comes and goes, can be confusing. If you trail out on the wrong end, you will merely trail to the spot where the cat spent the previous night, then probably stop for lack of scent.

Norm was off his horse, circling the kill away from me. Chink had trailed into the kill and was now working a line away beyond it, so we now knew where to concentrate our search for tracks. I started back along the path that Chink had followed and, at the top of a small ridge, found soil soft enough to display the lion's footprint. Interspersed with and under the tracks of the red dog were the broad, flat heel prints of a large tom lion.

I called to Norm that I had the track and that Chink was on the wrong end. He mounted and headed over the far ridge to catch the red dog and turn him around. Within minutes, Norm reappeared leading Chink with a short rope, followed by the pack of younger dogs. I began an excited cry of, "Here Chink, here it is. Here, here, here Chink." The strike dog came to me at a run, echoing my excitement with his staccato bark. As soon as I pointed at the track, he stuck his nose deeply into it, sucked in scent, and exploded into an enthusiastic chop. He worked the track rapidly, in the proper direction this time. As soon as he was lined out, Norm began to release the younger dogs, and the bawls of Rattler and Moonshine joined the staccato of Chink. Bonnie's shrill chop soon joined in. With four of them working, they moved rapidly over the ridge. We knew we were on last night's track, and my hopes rose that this would be a short chase. I should have known better.

We held the horses at a rapid walk in order to stay with the hounds. They moved the track southeast from the deer carcass, more or less in a straight line. The lion had not been hunting when he passed this point. He knew where was going. As was his habit, Chink had eased off on the track once Rattler, Moonshine, and Bonnie began to work it. He tended to play cheerleader after the task of locating a track was over.

The dogs took the track perhaps two miles to the southeast, using about an hour, then they seemed to bog down in the thick turbinella oak in the bottom of a wide draw. Their excitement said sign was hot, but they were milling in confusion. Chink set up a steady bark from the center of the thicket that almost, but not quite, said treed. I had heard this bark before and began to suspect that we were at the site of another kill.

I pushed my horse through the thick brush in a long circuit around the center of the dogs' activity, checking every bare patch of ground for an outgoing track. Norm worked his way directly to the dogs. Within a few minutes, he shouted to me that he had found the kill: a mule deer doe three to five years old. It was fresher than the carcass we had trailed from that morning and explained why the lion had not returned to the other kill site during the two preceding mornings. My hopes again rose that we would soon put the cat in a tree. With any luck at all, he should be brushed up near this kill. Perhaps we already had him jumped. If so, the dogs would soon find his departure route and push him to bay.

Once more, however, the lion did not perform as expected. The dogs worked in every direction but could not seem to take the track out. The lion had made several visits to the kill site, and his scent pervaded the area. The dogs simply could not sort out a single, departing line of tracks.

I continued my search of the area, working a circle some 100 yards out from the kill in order to avoid the clutter of lion and dog tracks near the kill site. Norm gathered the necessary information from the kill and joined me in the search for the track. The decomposed granite surface was tight and hard, and seeing a track would be difficult. We limited our search to patches of disturbed or frost-heaved soil where a depression might be made. Norm finally called me to him and pointed at a faint depression in the crumbled granite surface. "I think that's it," he said. "None of the dogs has been up here."

We couldn't see enough detail to be sure it was a lion track, but it was the best thing we had found, and it was the right size and shape. Norm's comment on the dogs meant two things: we weren't looking at a dog track, and the dogs had not checked this spot for scent. In lion hunting you learn to keep track of your dogs constantly. After you have worked a pack steadily for a year or so, you unconsciously know the position of every animal, even though the pack may number eight or more. This is essential in interpreting the sign you see. You will scrutinize a track-sized depression more closely, give more significance to a displaced pebble, if you know no dog has crossed the spot. You will use your eyes more sharply in places your best dogs have not covered. It's all part of the man-dog teamwork involved in hunting.

With one sniff in the depression, Chink acknowledged that it was lion and that it was fresh. We weren't sure it was the most recent path taken by the cat, but it was the best thing we had. We let the dogs work on it; their level of excitement told us we were probably right. Within a couple of hundred yards, we saw the track clearly in the soft surface of a saddle disturbed by bedding cattle. We were still on the right end.

A steep, rocky ridge and a difficult canyon crossing soon placed us far behind the dogs. I began to feel the familiar anxiety I always experience under such circumstances. It was conceivable, on such a fresh track, that the dogs would simply trail away and leave us. It had happened before. We topped a ridge and stopped to listen. We heard only the wind, buzzing insects, and jets overhead. Having a study area on a major east-west flight path for commercial jetliners had proven to be a nuisance. Even though the jets were thousands of feet high, their sound often screened the sound of hounds if we were trying to hear from a distance. In warmer weather, even the noises of insects can be a problem.

We had no way to know if the dogs were already out of hearing or simply bogged down on the track somewhere nearby and not giving voice. Situations like this can be exasperating. You do not know whether to charge ahead for a ridge or two in hope of hearing the dogs or to hold fast in hope of hearing the dogs. If you move on too rapidly, you may ride too far in the wrong direction, out of hearing. If the dogs are moving rapidly, you may never catch up.

You are, invariably, tempted to keep riding. Ninety percent of the time, this is the wrong thing to do. Silence usually signals a lost or overrun track. More often than not, when the dogs leave you at such a fast pace, their momentum will eventually cause them to overrun the track. You are usually better off sitting and quietly listening, dispelling your impatience by searching for tracks of the dogs and attempting to trail them up. Casting hurriedly about the country in search of the animals usually accomplishes little more than tiring horses and people.

In this case, we were wise and waited. We could see where the dogs had crossed the ridge and were able to work the track slowly into the bottom of the next draw. They seemed to head over the next ridge, so we topped it and stopped to listen. After some ten minutes, we finally heard Chink's voice in the thick bottom of the draw behind us. They had overrun, and we would have compounded the problem had we hurried ahead in search of them.

We found the dogs milling on a dry south-facing slope bisected by a large vein of white quartz. Air temperature was approaching sixty degrees, and the exposed soil and rock probably exceeded this temperature by another twenty degrees. Trailing was becoming more difficult. Chink had given up on the younger dogs and, dropping the role of cheerleader, began to search for the track. His intermittent barking said he was having some success.

He slowly moved the track back across the ridge we had just crossed: the lion had circled back on itself. When the track crossed another ridge top and entered heavy brush on a north slope, all of the dogs once again gave voice and moved rapidly along the contour of the canyon. They seldom put their noses to the ground here, taking scent from twigs and leaves of shrub oak or manzanita. The thick brush reduced the options available for direction of travel, so the dogs had to search less for the track. We were again hard-pressed to keep up.

Noon had come and gone, and we found ourselves in a succession of rapid trailing sprees followed by losses as the cat crossed open, bare slopes or made unpredictable turns. Trailing became slower, even on the cool slopes. Once or twice we considered giving up when the dogs failed to find the track for a half hour or more. Each time, however, just as were ready to call dogs and leave, Chink would open somewhere ahead, the young dogs would join him, and our hopes would again rise.

Sometime in the midafternoon the dogs trailed out onto a bare jeep road and immediately lost the track. We knew what had happened and knew that we might now be finished for the day. Lions, like coyotes, deer, and many other animals, will use primitive roads as trails. Roads usually follow gentler slopes and provide a path of least resistance through the country. Our cat had followed the road.

The dogs could not pick up the scent on the hot, packed surface. Judging by the angle at which we had hit the road, the cat had probably followed it to the south. I dismounted and began to examine the ground closely. I could not see any outline of a track but could see places where something had disturbed the fine layer of silt that lay sparsely over the harder surface. I could also see where deer had disturbed this surface, but their harder tracks left enough of an outline for identification.

It seemed, then, that our guess that the lion had continued south was right. The trick now was not so much to follow him but, since he was following the road, to find where he turned off. I worked slowly, seeing at intervals of several feet periodic faint smudges in the one-layered surface that hinted that a padded foot had passed this way. The dogs had gone to shade and were content to let me work for a change. Unless I could find a good track leaving the road, our hunt was over. They were tired and hot and would readily have followed us to the truck at this stage.

Norm, too, was content to let me do the tracking. In a situation such as this, two people working a track may be a handicap. It is often better for one person to work and the others stay back rather than tramp the ground with a mass search. Norm was basically a better tracker than I, but he was willing to let me work this one out. I was almost on hands and knees trying to see the faint smudges.

I continued for a hundred yards or so, crossing a small drainage and starting up its far side. Every few feet, I would see a faint disturbance. I could only assume that I was still seeing lion tracks. Finally I covered some fifty feet of road without seeing anything. I backed up to my last track and tried again to work from there. No luck. I checked the top of the next ridge, again seeing no visible sign. Either the ground through this stretch was accepting no track or the cat had turned off. I returned once more to the place I'd last seen sign and searched the roadside carefully. Perhaps I could find where he had departed. Again, no luck. Finally, I gambled. Odds were the cat would continue traveling in the direction he had been going when he had hit the road. I surveyed the roadside brush and terrain and picked what I thought would be the most likely departure route. I called Chink and pointed to the ground as if I had a track. He set to work and shortly opened on a scent. The other dogs once more joined in and slowly turned the track westward. I smiled at Norm and shrugged my shoulders. He knew I'd been lucky. At this point, if you're guiding dudes, you stay quiet and look wise. Your client thinks you're the greatest tracker that ever lived.

The track was tough through the afternoon, with Norm, Chink, or I finding it when the younger dogs bogged down. Warm sun and dry ground made trailing hard, but we never totally lost the track. We trailed into the deep shadow of a long, boulder-strewn mountain called Connell Hills—as rough a piece of terrain as anyone would ever hope to negotiate. The dogs continued up the rough face of the mountain over a route our horses could not follow. They seemed to move faster as they hit the protected slope. We turned northward and found a gentler ridge that kept us in sight and hearing of the dogs.

The trail led to a large bluff surrounded by massive granite boulders and thick chaparral on all sides. We could only watch the dogs from a distance. The sun was low in the sky. The February day was running out. We were in terrain we didn't relish negotiating after dark.

The dogs were milling in boulders and cracks surrounding the large bluff, seemingly bogged down once more. I was almost ready to call them in, if I could, and head down the mountainside. I was, in fact, begining to feel that we had waited too long and gone too far. Even though the day had been warm, we knew the night would bring temperatures well below freezing. We had sat beside a fire overnight on a mountainside before; we preferred not to do it again unless we had no choice.

As I opened my mouth to call, we heard Rattler bawl on the back side of the bluff and rapidly fade away to the south. The other dogs joined him and soon moved out of hearing. We had to circle to the top of the mountain and swing back down another ridge in order to parallel the movements of the dogs. Sunset was almost upon us when we reached the approximate point where we'd last heard the dogs and dismounted to listen. We were looking down a steep, rocky slope that led even further from our truck. For long moments, we heard nothing and began to fear the dogs had taken the lion out of our hearing. The speed with which they had faded from our hearing made us certain that they'd jumped him in the jumble at the base of the bluff.

Suddenly, we heard Bonnie's wild chop, moving fast around the base of the mountain. Moonshine soon joined in, and, within seconds, he began to bark treed. Bonnie turned back and joined him. In her excitement, she had overrun the tree. The voices of Chink and Rattler soon added to the melee and finally, the two Walker pups made their first sounds of the day.

I looked at Norm and shook my head. It would be dark, or nearly so, by the time we led our horses down the half-mile slope to the cat. We could be in for a night on the mountain if we dropped off that side.

"Those dogs have worked too hard," was Norm's only comment. "We can't leave them now."

We headed down the boulder-strewn slope. It was barely light enough to see when I tied my horse near the base of the juniper that the lion had climbed. The dogs maintained a constant din. The lion, a large male as we had surmised, was sitting in the highest crotch of the tree, some twenty feet from the ground, snarling his displeasure and indignity. I worked around until I could get a clear view of his head through the juniper limbs and confirmed what I had uneasily suspected all day—the cat was already marked.

"It's old Number 14," I called to Norm. He had approached from the downhill side and could not see the green plastic tag hanging from a rope around the cat's neck. "We won't have to handle him." If we could grab the dogs quickly, we might get off of this mountain and on a decent trail while we could still see.

I started for the dogs, and the lion left the tree. It and the dogs disappeared over a rocky ridge to the east. With them went our hope of leaving the rough country before dark, even though the cat treed again within a quarter mile. I topped a ridge and watched the tom double back on his track in the faint evening light, then calmly check out a couple of trees before selecting one to climb. I had always assumed lions treed only when pushed hard by dogs, but this one obviously selected a tree to his liking and climbed it at his leisure, while the dogs were still trying to unravel his backtrack. Several minutes passed before the dogs straightened the erratic track and discovered the cat. The barking started again.

It was dark by the time we necked the dogs and led them away. For a while, the faint glow of dusk allowed us to see the shapes of boulders and pick our way between the worst clumps, but, within a half hour, we could barely see where we were placing our feet. I stumbled, stopped, and sighed. Norm said, "We'd better build a fire. We'll have some moonlight later." We tied dogs and horses and gathered wood as best we could in the dark. The fire, once started, gave enough light to allow us to locate additional wood, and we were soon reasonably comfortable, sitting with our backs against a granite boulder.

An hour or so passed before the moon finally cleared the horizon. It was about two-thirds full and gave ample light for us to pick our way to the horse trail that led to the truck. In spite of the long route we had followed that day, we were within an hour's ride of the truck once we reached the trail. We loaded dogs and horses and were home by midnight. It had been a long day, and we had not marked a new lion.

CHAPTER SEVEN
GUIDES

In my lion hunting, I had the best of both worlds. I had the privilege of following the dogs, watching them work, treeing the cat, and as a hunter, even shooting lions—but they did not die. The work we did was strictly for the purpose of marking and studying lions. We shot them only with tranquilizers.

Historically, this has not been the purpose of lion hunting, nor is it the main purpose of lion hunts today. Even now, most hunters who seek lions do so to take home a trophy. The death of the lion is their goal. For those who hunt lions only once or twice in their lives, and who consciously and directly seek a lion, this can be accomplished only by hiring a guide and dogs.

A high percentage of people who develop a dog pack and learn to tree lions become guides. This has become even more the case in the past two decades as the value of lions as a big game trophy has increased, as efforts to control lions as predators have decreased, and as regulations governing lion hunting have become more restrictive.

People who in the past were legally able to take several lions per year are now confronted with annual bag limits of one lion per hunter per year. In some states, they may have to acquire a special permit by drawing in order to hunt lions at all. Restrictions on the circumstances under which lions can be taken for livestock damage have increased. Even treeing lions for the pleasure of working dogs, without shooting the cat, is restricted in most states. As a result of all of this, anyone who wants to keep good hounds must find legal ways to work their dogs. This usually leads to guiding.

As the previous sections have indicated, lion hunting is not a sport that can be approached casually. Hounds must be worked regularly to be good. They must be exercised almost daily, and ideally they should be hunted weekly. Young dogs cannot be trained unless they help tree lions. To function properly as a pack, hounds must be worked together. Guiding gives a legal basis for such work. It also helps to support the pack.

For lion hunting is not cheap. The terrain and climate in which hunting occurs demands the use of four-wheel-drive vehicles. A new four-wheel-drive pickup will represent a year's take-home pay for many of us. A pack of four dogs, two working dogs and two youngsters being trained, will cost a minimum of $50 to $75 per month to maintain. Horses and horse trailers can rapidly add $7500 to the capital cost of the operation, plus the cost of horse feed and care—another $50 to $75 per month per horse. Gas, travel, and time off from work all add their economic toll. Lion hunting is not a sport for poor people. Again, guiding helps pay the bills.

There are, as it were, degrees of guiding. While some hunters declare themselves a guide as soon as they catch their first lion (and I've known several licensed "lion guides" who had never seen a lion), the wiser neophytes test their skills and develop their technique by taking friends along for the hunt. The purpose may not be profit but rather expense sharing, companionship, or simply someone to take the lion legally so that the dog owner does not have to use up his permit, hence stop hunting. This latter problem depends upon the state in which the hunt occurs.

A high percentage of those who stay with hounds and hunting eventually declare themselves professionals. They may take ten years of practice or more in reaching this point. Many of these see guiding only as a sideline, a means to subsidize their sport and to write off hunting expenses on their tax returns. A few depend upon guiding for a high percentage of their total income, but virtually none make their entire livelihood from guiding, especially for lions.

Just as there are degrees of commitment to guiding, there are degrees of quality in guides and hunts. The best guides have adequate equipment and facilities to set up comfortable camps in lion country. They have their clients up and moving horseback by sunup or shortly after and into rugged lion habitat in search of a track. They have top dogs and top mounts, be they horses or mules, and they will tree lions on dry land or snow.

These are master hunters, and they may earn half of their annual income or more guiding for lions, black bear, and in season, other big game. From them, a hunter buys use of equipment, personal care, and unsurpassed knowledge of game and country. In Arizona, at least, a high percentage of such guides may own or work for a cattle ranch. Their original involvement in lion hunting may well have been as a result of livestock losses. They developed a pack to protect their possessions. At some point, they realized the dollar value of lions as trophies, and they began to subsidize their cattle operation with guiding.

Guiding and ranching fit well together. Horses need not stand idle between roundups. Some ranchers even allow their hounds to second as stock dogs. Hounds may not serve well to drive livestock, but in rough, brushy country, they can stop and hold a wild range steer at bay as well as any livestock dog breed. Moreover, ranch equipment and facilities such as horse trailers and line cabins serve well in guiding operations. And guiding keeps a rancher out on the ground among his stock.

Lesser quality guiding operations house clients in small-town motels, then run roads in surrounding lion country, on fresh snow, in search of a track. When a track is found, dogs are dumped and the hunt is on. Such a hunt will often occur on foot, and the client engaged in such an operation had best be in exceptional physical shape. By the time a hunter has waded knee-deep snow for a day or more to get to a tree, he will indeed have earned his trophy. Much is missed, however, in such a hunt as compared to the campout described above. The camp and its atmosphere are gone, the camaraderie around a campfire, the cold ride out in the morning, the opportunity to stay with the dogs while they cold trail, to be close when the lion is jumped, and possibly, to see the chase. Such things make a lion hunt memorable. Hunters who seek less—simply the opportunity to shoot a lion from a tree—miss the best parts of the hunt.

In guiding, as in all forms of business, there are those who operate at less than ethical levels—and those who will pay for less than ethical hunts. Some guides keep a list of hunters on standby. When a fresh track in the snow is found, or a fresh kill, a trip to the nearest phone gets a client on the way—sometimes from five hundred or more miles away. More often than not, the guide goes alone with the dogs and trees the lion, while a helper meets the client at the nearest airport and brings him to the tree. All the client does is pull the trigger, and killing a lion in a tree is a simple matter. Such clients have not hunted lions. Stories of their hunt will necessarily be lame lies. They might just as well have bought a tanned hide from a taxidermist.

Such guides, at least, do not delude their clients regarding the type of hunt they are getting. At the bottom of the list are the guides that do. These are the guides that hunt steadily between clients and take lions alive. They may even buy live lions from other unethical hunters. Prior to the advent of the tranquilizer gun, hunters often roped the cats in the tree, stretched, and tied them. Modern technology and drugs have made the job easier. The lions are held at a remote location until a client is on hand, then, by prearrangement with helpers, released at a given time and place, just moments ahead of guide, client, and dogs. The helpers disappear, the guide arrives and wisely states that this is a place where lions frequently cross. He sees the track, dumps the dogs, and ten to fifteen minutes later, the lion is treed. The client goes home with his trophy believing he has seen lion hunting at its best. In truth, it takes good lion hunters and a good organization to make such an operation work, but the client is cheated of the real hunt and excitement. He might as well have shot his neighbor's house cat.

To some extent, then, the quality of the hunt and its cost are inversely related to the ease with which a client gets a lion, or with the odds of taking one at all. Compared to most other forms of guided hunts, such as those for the various forms of mountain sheep, lion hunts are still relatively cheap. The hunter who flies in from L.A. is led to a tree by the guide's teenaged son, points his, or the guide's, rifle, and pulls the trigger may, at the time of this writing, pay five hundred to a thousand dollars for the privilege of shooting a lion. The "canned," guaranteed hunt with lion released ahead of the hunter will cost a bit more due to the expenses of catching and holding lions and of paying extra help. Since this type of operation is illegal, a cost covering the risk involved may also be hidden in the bill.

The real lion hunt, with full camp, a cook, a dude wrangler, horses, dogs, and top guide is the most expensive. It can run $200 to $250 per day per hunter, with a minimum of three to five days charged, regardless of how soon a kill is made. In some cases, a kill fee may be added on top of the daily guiding fee. The hunter who pays for such a hunt, however, knows why he is there. He expects nothing more from his guide than an all-out effort. If a lion is treed, fine. If not, camp, rides, scenery, camaraderie, and the chance to see top dogs and and trackers in action is worth the price.

Considering the overhead involved in maintaining dogs, horses, and so on, guided lion hunts are still among the least expensive hunts. They tend to be a bargain. Even the all-out camp hunt can be had for under two thousand dollars in most areas. Prices have been held down to some extent by the quickie hunts and by the fact that the lion is still considered a varmint, with no real value, by some hunters. Ranchers, using lion hunts as a sideline to their cattle operations, can also afford to keep prices low. Many see lion hunting, even guided hunts, as a means of protecting stock. Any money they make from a hunt is gravy.

This situation is changing slowly as lions come into their own as a trophy species. Also changing is the nature of the hunts. Nature buffs who have no desire to collect trophies but know that dogs are essential to see lions, are paying for nonconsumptive hunts. They may merely photograph the lion and demand its release. Such people will pay as much as a trophy hunter to see a lion. Hunters guiding such hunts can recycle lions, injuring nothing more than the animal's pride. Studies of lions throughout the West have demonstrated that treeing them with dogs does not cause them to vacate their home areas. Some ranchers are discovering that the lions on their ranches are worth as much as the calves they eat. They simply pass their profits up the food chain. Such an attitude flies in the face of tradition, but it may lead to more profitable ranching operations.

One of the myths surrounding the lion is that it is near extinction. All available evidence from studies in the western United States says this is not so. Historically, those species that have been given value as sporting animals have become the most secure. Hunters pay to maintain the species they want to hunt. Saving animals to be shot may not appeal to many, but it is a tried philosophy that gives positive value to many animals. This, perhaps, assures them space on our planet a while longer.

CHAPTER EIGHT
A Guided Hunt

I've portrayed in Chapter Six a hunt that I thought was near-perfect. It happened to be one in which we as biologists also performed as the principal hunters. It occurred near the end of our research efforts on the Spider Ranch, after I had spent five years under the tutelage of several of the best lion hunters in Arizona. That hunt was a sort of final exam for me, with the professors absent.

Many hunts occurred before that one in which success depended entirely upon the experience and judgement of the guide who was helping us on the study. Because he lived within commuting distance of the study area and because he ranked with the best, that guide was usually George Goswick.

This particular hunt was, I felt, unique, because it called more upon an almost mystical judgement on the part of the hunter than upon his tracking skills. It ended in the capture of a new, large tom. A less-experienced hunter might have never known a lion was near.

The hunt really started all wrong. George was scheduled to meet me at the Cross U Ranch headquarters, where I was living at the time. We planned to start early from there and trailer to a site on the rugged west side of the ranch, perhaps fifteen miles from headquarters. The time and distances involved made an early start essential.

I awoke about four and forced myself out of bed. We had been hunting steadily for several days, and I was feeling the wear of early mornings and long rides. George, too, must have been reaching that point, for he didn't show at the prescribed time. I wasn't particularly disappointed when an hour passed and he still hadn't arrived. A day in a warm abode, catching up on field notes (also called napping), really sounded good.

I helped feed horses, delivered my daughter to the school bus, and returned the eight miles to the ranch with relaxation fully in mind. I'd no more than pulled alongside my mobile home when George arrived with his normal complement of horses and dogs. By this time, it was pushing eight. The day would be too short to make the hunt we had planned.

We seriously considered scrapping the hunt entirely. George had been delayed by a horse that had escaped from his Prescott corrals and had proceeded to trot behind the paper boy on his morning rounds. Neither of us was thrilled about the prospect of hard saddles or barking dogs, but we felt it would be a shame to waste George's drive to the ranch. There was a small chunk of country immediately behind the ranch that had received little hunting attention, simply because it was so close. We decided to make a short ride up a rough draw called Wikieup Canyon. With luck, we'd find no track and could call it a day early.

But Murphy's Law is constant. If you don't want a lion, one will appear.

We worked slowly up the rim. The mid-December day turned out warm. The dogs were weary from several days of hunting. Our procession was one of laziness and virtual spring fever, with total non-accomplishment in mind. Unfortunately, the dogs were more dedicated in research than we.

I think either Speed or Maggie opened first. These were George's old strike dogs. Even when exhausted, they never forgot entirely why we were afield. The track was not fresh, however. It seemed to be merely scattered scent remaining in the cooler sites under junipers. The dogs opened here and there, but no real trailing was in progress. Chink, my red dog, honored the barks of George's dogs, but showed no excitement about the track. He and George's tree dog, Yeller, finally grew bored and worked their way down a talus slope into the canyon bottom.

At this stage, you need to know something about Yeller. He wasn't a normal lion dog. If he knew how to work a track, he never let it be known. That was work for the hounds. Yeller was an aristocrat of sorts. His breeding was a bit of a mystery. He may have had some hound in his background, but there was no way to be sure. George said he knew of Doberman in the dog's lineage, but he really wasn't sure what else. Yeller had been acquired for use as a stock dog, rather than for lions. But he learned about lions and developed his own special place in the pack. He was a professional tree dog.

On any given hunt, during most of the day, Yeller would be lounging along in the shade of one of the horses, seemingly unaware of any track the hounds might be working. However, let that track lead us into one of the granite boulder piles common on the Spider-Cross U complex or let it take us along a steep canyon with brushy rimrocks for sides, and Yeller would silently disappear. Yeller didn't trail lions, he hunted them. He let the hounds get him close; he knew where lions would lie up at midday; and he searched for lions. His athletic build, undoubtedly a derivative of his Doberman lineage, allowed him to move easily through the roughest rims and boulders. He searched these areas hole by hole and brush pile by brush pile until he jumped the cat. He then drove it to tree. Innumerable times, when we were working slowly along behind hounds pounding a cold trail, George would stop and ask, "Where's that yeller dog?" More often than not, if we stopped to listen between the bawls of the trailing hounds, we would soon hear Yeller barking treed a half mile ahead.

This day, Yeller and Chink broke off on their own short foray into the canyon bottom. Perhaps Yeller had a mystical inkling of a cat's presence. I came to suspect him of such abilities. More likely, however, he simply recognized the rough brushy rim of Wikieup as a likely place for a lion to spend the midday hours. He did his usual thing and went searching. Chink tagged along because the scent on the canyon rim wasn't warm enough to be interesting.

They had hardly hit the canyon bottom when both dogs broke into a barrage of chopping barks and dashed up canyon at full speed for about two hundred yards. Then all became silent except for an occasional yip from one of the two dogs below.

The other hounds worked their way off the rim and joined Chink and Yeller, milling about an area less than a hundred yards in diameter. Every so often a hound would bawl or yip, but none of them seemed able to move a track out of the area. None of them spoke as if the track were fresh.

Now, George Goswick isn't known for being verbose. If you learned anything from him, you did it by watching. I don't think he felt any need to hide the secrets of his trade, but he obviously didn't need to prove his knowledge by talking about them. He simply caught lions, and if you trailed along and watched, you could slowly learn at least something about how he did it.

George sat on his horse, gazing over the rim at the dogs in the bottom. He gave them time to work, but nothing definitive happened. The dogs continued to mill about and periodically yip or bawl. I thought we would call them off and go on (or better yet, return home; the warm sun was making the thought of a nap attractive).

Finally, George dismounted and found a comfortable spot against a rock where he could absorb sun and watch the dogs. He lit a cigarette and smoked leisurely, crushing the butt on the bare rock beside him. I expected him to call the dogs, but he continued to scan the area below intently. I'd found a good spot in the sun, too, so I dozed and waited. Maybe, I figured, he had decided to kill the day this way. At least we wouldn't have to ride any further from the ranch.

A half hour passed, and George lit another cigarette—a sign that we were going to wait a while longer. Even through my lazy contentment, curiosity and impatience got the best of me. "What's going on, George?" I asked.

"Best I can figure, we've got a lion in a tree down there somewhere," was his answer.

I wasn't about to question the judgement of anyone of George's stature in lion hunting, not out loud, anyway, but I had been in on quite a few cats by this time. I knew this wasn't the way they were caught. For one thing, we hadn't trailed a lion yet. Any lesser hunter than George I would have accused of malingering and nursing a hangover. But I knew he was serious.

So I shut up and waited.

Finally, George stirred and said, "Why don't you take these horses and find a trail you can lead them down? I'll drop off here on foot and see what I can find."

It took me about half an hour to head a side canyon and lead our horses down a narrow stock trail. Nothing had changed when I reached the area where the dogs, and by now, George were searching. Some of the dogs had given up and were asleep in a patch of sunshine on the canyon slope. Others continued to check scent beneath the mixed ponderosa pine, alligator juniper, and Gambel oak overstory.

George waved me over to a small patch of snow lying in a spot the sun did not reach. "There's a lion here," he said. Amidst the multitudinous tracks left by the milling dogs, there was a single print with the unmistakable three-lobed heel of a lion. It appeared nearly as fresh as the tracks of the dogs.

George methodically continued to search the tree tops in the area, and I followed suit for a while. Another half hour passed, and I was about to decide the whole thing was silly. I found an exposed, warm slope, already partially occupied by snoozing hounds, and leaned back against the hill side. There may have been a lion here sometime, but George's persistence in the search was totally out of proportion to the strength of the evidence. Even the dogs were losing interest.

I was drifting into sleep when George's voice, unchanged in tone from any other words he had spoken that day, penetrated the haze of my impending nap, "Here he is."

And he was. I've seldom given lions much credit for intelligence. I think they are basically an instinctive beast, but this old male was compressed, in as obscure a manner as possible, into the crotch of a half-dead Gambel oak. Both of us had passed under him more than once in our searching. He was hidden as well as a 150-pound cat can hide amidst bare limbs. I think we'd missed him to this point because we expected him to be crouched in one of the more protective evergreens.

Whatever the case, he had escaped both us and some of the best dogs in the West for some two hours while we searched within the range of his vision. I would have moved on long before; I suspect 99 percent of people who run dogs would have. Only a hunter with the sensitivities of a lifetime of hunting, such as Goswick, would have the strength of conviction to

66

continue his search. Success, in this case, depended not upon skill in trailing or even upon exceptional dogs. It depended upon a knowledge of the cats that few people will have the time or persistence to acquire.

CHAPTER NINE
Deer Hunters and Ranchers

 Two groups have historically been antilion: ranchers and deer hunters. Their motivation is the protection of ungulates that they want for themselves. The rancher has led the fight against predators in the West. Deer hunters, as a separate group, have not held the strong feelings of enmity toward predators characteristic of ranchers, but have either supported lion control or been passive when it occurred.

The rancher alone is in a position to have his livelihood affected by lions and has traditionally sought government aid for predator control. For a nonrancher, the relationship of the rancher to predators is hard to understand. He seems to be in the position of a person who parked his car on a railroad crossing, then sued the railroad company for the vehicle's destruction. The predators were there first; the rancher knew they were there and would cause trouble. Involved here is a basic life philosophy—that of drastically modifying the world for the sake of a few individuals—that many find hard to understand. We question whether this planet exists to serve the human species alone.

In the case of the rancher, this becomes even harder to accept, for his very lifestyle bespeaks freedom and independence. He usually flaunts his disdain for big government, but he grazes public land, and he asks for control of predators on those lands. More recently, some ranchers led the so-called Sagebrush Rebellion in an effort to convert the public domain of the West to state or private lands. In so doing, they hoped to gain more control of grazing levels and of predators. Of course, land outside the public domain is in danger of subdivision. Thus, in many ways, the rancher often seems to threaten the very wildness that makes the West unique.

Those of us who value public lands and the wildlife they sustain tend, therefore, to maintain vigilance against the most "western" symbol of all: the Cowboy. In so doing, however, we must seek to base our caution upon a background of truth. This has not always been the case where issues surrounding predators have been concerned.

Our research on Spider Ranch demonstrated that the ranchers' problem with lions is, in places, very real. Lions eat cattle and sheep in appreciable numbers at times. Control (efforts at eradication) historically has been the most direct, although not necessarily the simplest or cheapest means of dealing with lions. In recent years ranchers have fallen into disrepute because of their impact on wolves, coyotes, and grizzly bears. We must take care, however, in judging those past acts in the light of our times, and perhaps the rancher needs to not judge modern environmentalists in the light of those times to which he clings.

Analyzing the rancher as he relates to lions is a complex process. For one thing, there is no average rancher. Nor do ranchers belong to a single category. Very few of the old, single-family ranches still exist. Such ranches have been handed down from father to son. The generation running them is the second or third on a piece of land. Ranchers in this category probably feel most strongly about predators and cling most tenaciously to the hope of predator elimination. They are still attached to the early Christian ethic that sees domestication of wild areas as a human duty, and they have grown up on the land. Their attitudes are deeply inscribed, and they object strongly when outsiders suggest that their cattle management, range management, or predator management should change. Because of their closeness to the land, their experience and convictions are difficult to shake. Perhaps asking them to change is asking too much. They truly come from another time and another set of values. They will probably precede the lion in extinction.

At the other extreme, however, is the large ranch corporation. This is usually a big-city group with holdings in many areas of finance. Ranches are bought as long-term investments in land, short-term tax write-offs, and weekend playgrounds for members and associates. On the surface, such businesses should not be deeply concerned with predation. Large profits from livestock are not their goal. More often than not, however, such ranches are still managed by local people, very often a member of the original family in the area. If the original family leaves, the ranch may be managed by cheaply bought personnel who know little of ranching. Highly capable corporate managers seem to be consistently poor at selecting ranch managers. I think this may be because they see all land as something to develop and civilize. Wildness becomes expendable, and sustained progressive cattle management is not always a goal. They do not differentiate between ranch managers and caretakers.

Between these extremes run an array of other types of ranch owners, from retired mechanics who lay out their life savings as a down payment on an operation too small to give them a living, to professionals who have made it big in medicine or law, then retire to a ranch. With such a great variety of backgrounds to assess, one wonders if an accurate picture of today's rancher can be drawn, but I think there is a common element that binds these newcomers, and thus, aligns their thinking. I believe it helps explain the sometimes archaic attitude of newly arrived ranchers toward predators and toward the land.

This common element is, I suspect, the cowboy image. This is the greatest of all American male dreams; the ultimate machismo of America. Owning a ranch and being a real cowboy is the American form of "having arrived." Remington, Russell, and Roosevelt, followed by movie and television westerns, have imprinted this image so strongly on Americans that it has become the subconscious goal of a high percentage of American males, and males from other countries as well. Doctors buy ranches after they succeed in their chosen specialties. Airline captains slip away to ranches between flights and don chaps, boots, hats, and even Colts. Corporate giants buy ranches, Mafia leaders buy ranches, men who have succeeded in other arenas consistently shed the image that gave them their success and revert to cowboying. And they look with adulation on the uneducated hand who really grew up on a horse, winters in a line shack, and makes

$300 a month plus beef. This force, I think, consolidates the thinking of all who enter ranching. It also influences many (myself included) who find it cheaper just to buy the hat, boots, and chewing tobacco—the image—and forget the ranch.

The second antilion group, deer hunters, is even more difficult to characterize than ranchers (and, obviously, overlap occurs between these two groups). Deer hunters come from all walks of life, equipped with all sorts of knowledge, experience, and ability. Although much of their recreation and lifestyle may center around an outdoor image, they can, in truth, be deer hunters for only a very short time each year. They, too, seek a unified image, and that image is one of success.

Say what you will about the quality of the outdoor experience, of camping, of enjoying the quest; the deer hunter seeks to kill a deer. I believe that much of his purpose for hunting is to reaffirm his abilities in the woods. He seeks to assure himself that, if all of the systems our modern society has developed to provide food and security should fail, he could still make it. Even more important is returning to his community with a symbol of this ability: the carcass of a deer.

It is here that, in seeking the demise of predators, the hunter has missed the point. He has tried to find ways to make deer hunting easy. He has applied the mechanistic approach of his society to his symbol of independence from it and has asked, once more, that that society, via predator control, make things easy for him. In so doing, he is subverting his whole purpose for being afield.

What we really must assess here is whether any validity exists in the claims of those who request control of lions. We must distinguish clearly between the motives of the hunter and the rancher. The rancher, whatever his origin, is seeking a lifestyle. If he fails due to lion predation on his stock, he loses both self-esteem and money. The deer hunter is seeking a reaffirmation of an atavistic skill. If he fails to get a deer because a lion ate it first, his loss is one of inner prestige and security. Financial loss is not a serious consideration. The question, now, is do they, in the reality of nature, have reason to blame lions for these losses? When questioned this way, perhaps evidence says that they do, with qualification.

Through the environmental surge of the seventies, the reality of ranchers' losses to predators was severely questioned by many. The only people with direct experience in the area of livestock losses to predators were the ranchers themselves, or perhaps state or federal animal-control people. The latter were even more suspect than ranchers in the environmentalists' eyes, because their very livelihood depended upon killing predators. Objective information was scarce and had inherent biases that made interpretation difficult. Because of the difficulty in studying lions, objective data have accumulated slowly, and to some extent, these objective data have added to the confusion. Those who oppose the utilitarian attitudes of hunters and ranchers have capitalized on this. In recent years, the preservationists have done much to modify the concept of cougar.

CHAPTER TEN
Preservationists

 I remember a meeting some eighteen years ago between the Game Branch and the Research Branch of the Arizona Game and Fish Department. The research biologists had presented results and recommendations for studies of their respective species. Management personnel had expressed their immediate information needs. A question came from the moderator of the meeting, a gentleman long-since retired, regarding any new study needs that anyone might foresee.

A young biologist, sensitive to issues growing in his locality, asked, "How about lions and bears?"

The moderator, red-faced, erupted with, "It'll be a cold day in hell when we spend money on lion or bear research in this state." At that time, this administrator's dealings with the preservationist front had been limited. In less than a year, we were politically forced, largely by a group of middle-aged, nonhunting women, to design a study on lions. Bears followed a year later with little internal resistance.

This, perhaps, illustrates how rapidly the preservationists gained influence during the late sixties. Wildlife management agencies, comfortable with their relationships with hunters and ranchers, were suddenly challenged over their liberal attitudes toward killing of predators. In general, they reacted with hostility.

Coming from hunters' ranks, I still subconsciously react to the preservationist point of view as a threat, if I'm not careful. As a result, I may not always deal objectively with those who would totally protect animals. Basically, I find them and the antigun groups frequently attempting to limit activities that I enjoyed immensely, without hurting anyone, throughout my youth. I resent their advocacy of a mold I'd rather not accept. I suspect that the human species has an ontogenetic process in behavior patterns that each individual must live through. Young males of our species are basically predators from roughly ten years of age through their mid-thirties or early forties. Thwarting this predacious behavior as it relates to other animal species may redirect it toward humans, creating economic, if not physical, predation. In fact, I suspect that some of the extreme, almost terrorist-style, efforts of activists in the preservation movement is itself a redirection of human predation. Only the future will tell us whether this is a better use of the drive.

Like all of the other interest groups associated with lions, preservationists come in many forms. At one end of the spectrum are individuals who feel so much compassion for all living beings that they cannot conceive of killing either for sport or for personal gain. My comments above notwithstanding, I identify with these feelings more and more as I age. This may be part of the above-mentioned behavioral ontogeny. I have already hunted. Or it may be due to the fact that I've caught a bullet or two in my life and know how it feels. Whatever the cause, I seldom hunt anymore.

In spite of these shifting feelings, however, I remember how much I once enjoyed hunting, and I know that humans are so high on the food chain that we cannot exist without killing or displacing other organisms. Whatever our individual compassion for other species may be, we can be pure at this end of the preservationist spectrum only if we dissociate ourselves from our own bodies. As one old game warden put it, "Everyone truly believing in protectionism should hold their breaths for thirty minutes." But life goes on.

At the other end of the preservationist spectrum are those attached to the cause simply for personal gain, be it money, image, or power. Any issue that arouses human emotion will attract such parasites. They can be identified by the fact they spend their days keeping issues alive rather than seeking solutions. Their sustenance depends upon the continuation, not resolution of problems. Unfortunately, these individuals frequently maneuver themselves into administrative positions for organizations representing the preservationist cause.

Between these extremes lie all sorts of individuals. The most visible are the activists who seem to need a cause to validate their lives. They drift from issue to issue, yielding temporary support to the fad of the day. Less visible are those who truly espouse the preservationist viewpoint and spend their lives advocating changes in wildlife laws and regulations. Most of these, through education and practical political experience, usually assume moderate positions that give consideration to the desires of others. They become the most effective supporters of the preservationists' goals.

Mixed throughout all of this are those who have no strong feelings in the matter but will contribute funds and verbal support to any cause that sounds good. Such folks seldom take time to learn facts surrounding an issue, but they can be a major factor, at least financially, in keeping issues alive.

These concerns and criticisms aside, the impact of preservationists on the whole predator issue, including lions, has probably been beneficial. Americans definitely needed to review longstanding policies and attitudes toward predators, and preservationists have clearly forced such a review. The recent studies of lions would not have occurred were it not for preservationist pressures.

As a biologist, I applaud the preservationists' conservatism in wildlife management. We must, as the human species takes more space on this planet, approach exploitation of any fellow species with due caution and concern for its continued existence. We must also question our relationship with other species. Overconfidence that the earth was designed for the sole benefit of humans is perhaps our greatest weakness.

However, as a professional working with all human elements interested in wildlife, I have found the absolute moral self-righteousness of some of the more extreme preservationists to be annoying. I feel that they at times obstruct even positive efforts in understanding other species. Efforts a few years back by one of the more radical preservationist groups to eliminate the Pittman-Robertson program in wildlife research is an example. This program, supported by taxes on arms and ammunition, has supported virtually all of the research on huntable wildlife in our country over the past fifty years. Those opposing it contended that it studied animals only for the benefit of the hunter, therefore should be eliminated. They made no effort to create similar funds to study non-game species.

The overriding theme of these extreme groups has been that hunting or control of any wild animal population is evil. With this absolute as a guiding force, they have tended to use any ploy to win. In recent years, as a result, they have lost credibility and impact. Unfortunately, in the public eye (an increasingly urban public eye), any of us who exhibit concern for wildlife are now placed in the ranks with these extremists. These groups have thus weakened the environmental surge that was so strong in the seventies and have helped to send us pell-mell into the urban materialism of the eighties. I'm afraid wildlife and wildlands will suffer while we are regrouping.

In reality, biologists have created many of our own problems with preservationists. The oversimplified biology that we spoon-feed the lay public is frequently turned back upon us, and we have to eat our own words. We too often pretend to know more than we do. Preservationists have been quick to grasp and use principles that support their cause. And they have learned of our ignorance.

Early in the environmental movement, many individuals interested in wildlife, hunters and preservationists alike, developed concern over species that might be verging on extinction. This concern was well founded with species such as the whooping crane, the California condor, the ivory-billed woodpecker, the black-footed ferret, and an host of other creatures that were critically low in numbers. Similar concern was expressed for the lion, based partly upon its apparent total disappearance (with the exception of Florida) east of the Mississippi. This, combined with the innate cryptic nature of the species, led to speculation regarding its status throughout the West. By the mid-sixties, the preservationists were gathering their forces to protect the lion. In Arizona, this (supported, I might add, by many individuals from the ranks of guides and sport hunters) forced the state legislature to reclassify the lion from unprotected predator to presumably managed big game. These same pressures created research on the species. What we then called "little old ladies in tennis shoes" had been effective. They made us stop and look.

These preservationists heralded a concept called the balance of nature. Taken to its extreme, it held that intervention by humans, especially control or hunting of predators, upset the internal regulating mechanisms of nature that keep both predator and prey populations stable through time. This idea stemmed from the writings of early biologists, particularly those dealing with raptors and their impact on rodents. It has been applied to complex situations such as those involving lions in a form that is grossly oversimplified.

Related to this, another argument used by preservationists against hunting or predator control was the sanitation theory. This claimed, in its simplest form, that predators take only the weak, halt, or lame prey, eliminating them from the gene pool, hence benefitting the prey population in the long run. This derived from Darwin's theory of natural selection and was the cornerstone of early evolutionary theory. Results of early studies in relatively simple predator-prey complexes, such as wolf-caribou relationships, have been used to support sanitation as a concept and therefore, again, to oppose human intervention against predators. It has been applied in efforts to protect the lion.

To date, the impact of preservationists has been mixed, but I think it has been positive as regards the lion. Hunters, ranchers, and biologists may find preservationists threatening, but they have asked questions that we have been forced to answer. No group that encourages new knowledge can be all bad.

The contradictory viewpoints of the rancher, hunter, and the preservationist ultimately converged upon those of us who try to understand the interactions of humans and other animals. Insofar as our assimilation of facts is justly heard and our recommendations heeded, biologists become the main purveyors of the concept of cougar.

SECTION THREE

A
BLENDING OF
VIEWPOINTS

CHAPTER ELEVEN
Research

 As early as 1937, Frank Hibben wrote a bulletin on lions after hunting with several of the best lion hunters in Arizona and New Mexico. He checked the stomach contents of lions killed by these hunters. Only two percent of the lions he checked had eaten livestock. Nearly all held deer remains. Unfortunately, the area he covered was so broad that the conditions under which he worked were somewhat ill-defined. The ratios of cattle to deer in the areas he hunted were not known. He did not state how many cattle-free ranges his efforts covered. Nonetheless, his approach was an important beginning.

Stanley P. Young published *The Puma* in 1946. This was an excellent summary of knowledge regarding the lion to that date, and it included an abundance of food habits analyses. Much of Young's information was derived from files of federal trappers who worked areas where ranchers reported problems. As a result, one might think that his results would be somewhat biased. As with Hibben's work, Young's summary of lion use of livestock could not define clearly the exact conditions or prey availability under which it was compiled. Ratios of natural to domestic prey were not known. At any rate, Young, who admired the lion, noted fairly heavy use of cattle and sheep, particularly in Arizona and New Mexico. His figures suggested that lions, at least in some places, might eat more beef than Hibben had found to be the case.

W. Leslie Robinette noted a fairly high usage of domestic sheep by lions in Utah and Nevada, but deer, again, were the principal food. His data, however, were taken via stomach sample analysis using lion stomachs taken by animal-control personnel during the fifties. The data were, thus, strongly biased toward animals taken from livestock kills.

The first effort at studying lion predation under well-defined conditions occurred in the late sixties and early seventies. Taking Hibben's and Young's approach a technological step forward, Maurice Hornocker and his associates used tranquilizer guns and radio-telemetry on lions treed by dogs. They spent eight years studying movements, killing behavior, and social behavior of lions in the Idaho Primitive Area. They defined prey availability more precisely than any previous workers had done. Their work, however, focused upon the lion in a remote wilderness area. Livestock were not present. To no one's real surprise, they found lions eating deer and elk. They concluded, however, that lions, though uncontrolled, were not preventing prey species from increasing in number.

Once the Idaho workers had pointed the way to successful lion research, studies began in several western states. As results of these become available, they continue to illustrate the diversity of situations in which the lion lives and the variety of interactions between lions and prey, either native or domestic, that is possible. Ours was one of several studies that started about this time.

We began our efforts to study lion populations and predation in the Sycamore Canyon Primitive Area of Arizona in 1970. Our methods emulated Hornocker's, but we worked where cattle existed and where ranchers claimed a history of losses to lions. Ranchers' problems, countered by the claims of preservationists, were the reason we studied the cats. As is so often the case, a seemingly negative conflict created positive effort.

For a full year after we started, the study was a failure. We did not capture a single cat. In retrospect, this is probably fortunate, because we have since learned that the initial study area was not representative of the habitats where problems with lions and livestock actually exist. Our results there, if applied statewide, would have been misleading.

Regardless of the ultimate outcome, however, I was under pressure. Another lionless winter and I would probably be removed from the project as a total incompetent. That is a level of failure no one wants to confront. George Goswick was my rescuer. Disillusionment with Sycamore Canyon as a study area had led us to move to Spider Ranch. George was the best known of local houndsmen, and he agreed to help us on the study. On the third day that he guided us on the Spider Ranch, he treed a lion, and, after a year of frustration, I had a chance to do my biological thing.

The lion, a young mature female as it turned out, treed first in a small juniper on the north rim of a mesa overlooking Smith Canyon. I unleashed my pouch of capture equipment from behind the cantle and proceeded, amidst the chaos of baying hounds and excited horses, to try to dart the cat. I had loaded two separate darts at the beginning of our hunt. One dart was charged with enough drug to take an average-sized female; the other was loaded for a mature male. This, I hoped, would speed up operations at the tree. As the study progressed, I learned that this approach was a a mistake. The drug evaporated in the darts and acted as a glue on the injection mechanism. Darts loaded and carried too long would simply not inject. We had to load dosages at the tree.

This, however, did not become a problem on the day in question. I had just fully unpacked the equipment and loaded the pistol when the lion decided it wanted a better tree and left. Pursued by the dogs, she bailed off into the canyon and soon the baying of dogs could again be heard amidst a clump of bottomland cottonwoods and sycamores. I pushed the dart out of the barrel of the air gun (for safety's sake), repacked the gear, and spent twenty long minutes picking my way down the steep canyon wall to where George, dogs, and lion were waiting.

This time the cat had chosen a large, white-barked sycamore. It was the kind of tree I would learn with experience not to accept as a darting site. It was virtually unclimbable by humans, and the lion peered down from its uppermost branches, silhouetted by a brilliant Arizona sky. At this stage, however, simply getting a dart in a cat was of paramount importance to me. I again unpacked gear, loaded the pistol, and moved into position.

The pistol I carried was a standard piece of capture equipment for the time—a modified pellet gun powered by carbon dioxide cartridges. Give proper care, it worked reasonably well, but it did have periodic problems. For one thing, it was affected by the vagaries of temperature. When cold, the gas in the chamber contracted, and the gun lost power. When hot, it became supercharged. In addition to this, its power tended to vary inversely with the number of shots taken from a particular gas cartridge. With a fresh cartridge, the gun had spunk; after fifteen to twenty shots, it began to drop off. It was a tool that definitely required the skills of an artisan.

As a final handicap, the neoprene O-rings sealing the gas chamber on the gun occasionally dried out and developed leaks. This would result in no power at all and a tendency to leak the gas out of cartridges as fast as they could be replaced.

I had practiced with the gun extensively and felt that I knew its capabilities. I had started the hunt with a fresh cartridge. I was an experienced handgun shot. My confidence was high as I centered the front blade of the sights on the large muscle of the lion's front shoulder and squeezed the trigger. The gun went off with a sickly thump, and the dart flew about six feet above the barrel (I was shooting nearly straight up), peaked, then turned and fell back in my direction! I dodged out of its way, feeling like an artillery man with his missile gone astray. The dart bounced into a low oak thicket and disappeared. The lion decided things were getting a bit weird, and once more, left with dogs in hot pursuit. George mounted and hurriedly followed.

I was left behind with one missing dart, one overloaded dart, and a hyper horse objecting strenuously to having been left by the crowd. I began to search for the first dart, but quickly gave that up as the dogs once again began barking treed about a quarter-mile upstream. Hastily, I disassembled the second dart, reduced its charge, changed gas cartridges in the gun, threw gun and gear into my saddlebags, and charged up the canyon, hoping the lion would hold for just a bit longer.

By the time I reached the new tree, George was calmly sitting against a nearby sycamore and was halfway through a cigarette. Lions were nothing new to him, but I suspect that darting was beginning to be entertaining. I wondered if he was already wishing for the good old days of shooting lions with bullets.

The cat was in a large alligator juniper that had a central

crotch about four feet up and large, almost-horizontal limbs radiating from the crotch. The lion was at the end of one of these limbs, twelve feet from the ground. Just as I dismounted, a yearling pup belonging to George jumped into the crotch of the juniper and began to work its way out along the branch. I expected George to react, thinking that the dog was headed for certain death if it got too close. The pup moved swiftly out the limb, ignoring its narrowness, and began to bark literally in the face of the lion. The big cat snarled and struck with claws extended. The dog never ceased its barking as it dodged sideways, immediately lost its footing, and fell to the ground. It hit flat on its side with a resounding thud that temporarily stopped its barking.

George squashed his cigarette on a nearby rock, smiled up at me from his seat under the sycamore, and said, "That's twelve." The pup resumed its frantic bay, scrambled to its feet, jumped into the crotch of the tree and started its thirteenth trip out the limb.

I quickly loaded the gas pistol once more and sighted down its barrel at the lion. I wasn't perfectly steady by this time, but the distance was short, and the sights stayed well within the large target offered by the lion's ham. I squeezed. The gun fired with vigor and the dart departed at high velocity, passing a good foot over the back of the cat and disappearing into a thicket of dense six-foot manzanita fifty yards up the hill and across the canyon. The lion once again decided to move.

To keep the story from becoming tedious, suffice it to say that we eventually had to go back down the creek, search until we found the first dart, clean it, recharge it, and yet again approach the lion. This time it was in a small juniper, and I approached very closely, climbing to within about six feet of the animal. At that range, idiosyncracies of the gun could not create a miss. In spite of all, we ultimately marked the cat and fitted it with a radio-collar.

After a year of increasing anxiety, I slept the sleep of renewed hope that night (albeit nervous hope), and George, I'm sure, took stories back to his ranch—stories regarding the wonders of modern technology, the likes of which no hunter had ever given him before.

Needless to say, the whole study effort was not a repeat of the above. We gradually learned what we were about and began to catalog the data we sought. At the end of five years on the Spider-Cross U complex, we moved on to the North Kaibab and evaluated the impact of lions on deer populations there. The results of our eight years of effort have been duly published in appropriate reports and symposia proceedings.

The initial work in Arizona, perhaps, represented the opposite end of the spectrum from the Idaho study. We attempted to reproduce, insofar as local conditions allowed, the work of Hornocker on an area where cattle as well as deer were potential prey. The deer density was relatively low in relationship to carrying capacity of the range. The cattle operation involved year-long calving on open range in lion country.

Lions were protected from hunting on the area for five years. This was necessitated by the easy accessibility of the study area to hunters. The time and effort involved in marking lions was too great to risk losing them. In addition to this, we needed to view lion-prey relationships where lions were uncontrolled to provide a baseline for potential future studies involving hunted populations. As in the Idaho work, part of our job was to locate kills, the carcasses of animals killed, presumably for food, by lions. These are usually the carcasses of large animals such as deer. In Arizona, they were also the carcasses of cattle.

Such kills aren't easy to find. Lions seldom exist in densities higher than one lion per ten to twenty square miles for any extended time. They average about one kill per week, most of which they consume. Coyotes and ravens usually dispose of uneaten remains. The odds of being in the right place at the right time to document a kill are thus quite low.

These odds are driven even lower by the fact that lions hide their kills. The terrain they occupy and hunt is rough and brushy. They tend to pull carcasses under low-hanging trees and into dense brush, then bury them with debris. A high number of kills can be found only with the help of good dogs, radio-marked lions, and personnel who have a background of spotting lion-killed prey.

Such a background doesn't develop without setbacks. We learned early in our efforts that trying to find radioed lions from the ground, for the sake of studying movements and locating kills, was time consuming and unproductive. Frustrations in trying to locate radioed lions from our pickups or high-points are exemplified by the fact that we once spent the better part of an afternoon tracking a signal that we ultimately realized was emanating from our own pickup. Rough roads had activated a spare collar. At this point, we decided that tracking from aircraft was essential.

Actually, we used two techniques in locating lion kills. All kills found in the process of trailing lions with dogs for the purpose of marking were tallied, as were kills located by making deliberate searches in areas used by radio-marked lions. We attempted to clump our aerial radio-tracking efforts into thirty-day clusters, thereby knowing when a lion had remained immobile for two or more days in succession. We took such immobility to signal a possible kill and searched these areas carefully. This approach worked reasonably well, allowing us to locate approximately eighty fresh lion kills over a five-year period.

As we began to search for lion kills on and around Spider Ranch, we learned via our own observations and through discussions with ranchers why uncertainty existed regarding the real impact of lions on both wild and domestic prey. For one thing, considerable differences of opinion existed in the ranks of ranchers themselves. Some of this was due to the ability and inclination of the rancher to find kills; some was due to the habitat in which he worked.

Within twenty-five miles of Prescott, Arizona, for example, we dealt with three different life-long ranchers. One who ran cattle in a virtual lion haven, all boulders and brush, lost calves constantly to the big cats. Interestingly enough, he felt coyotes had little or no impact on his calf crop. A rancher on an adjoining range had a well-managed herd of registered herefords, running in rolling grasslands. The only lion loss he ever experienced was a fluke. He complained constantly, however, of coyotes killing his registered calves or bobbing their tails.

The last was a third-generation rancher. He had grown up on the very land he rode daily, and it was lion habitat. We approached him one day for permission to cross his deeded land to search an area we felt might hold a kill made by one of our radioed females. He gave permission willingly but did not offer to accompany us, even though the potential kill was on his range. His parting statement was, "In forty years of riding this country, I've never seen a calf killed by a lion." Fifteen minutes later we were standing over the half-buried carcass of a calf bearing his brand. We knew of others that had died similarly.

In documenting these kills, we did our best to determine whether a lion had actually done the killing or not. Tradition held that lions always killed their own meat, but the limited literature available and our continuing discourse with experienced houndsmen, disclosed that exceptions, while rare, did exist. Of the kills we located on Spider Ranch, only three were cases of lions feeding on carrion. In two of these instances, the carcasses were full-grown cattle, animals larger than the lions would normally attempt to kill. The other case was unique and perhaps shows something of the adaptability of the cat.

Jim Higgs was an old school mate of mine. He was also the District Wildlife Manager for Arizona Game and Fish Department in the area surrounding our lion study area. He had worked in lion country throughout his career and knew something of their behavior. As a result, he was almost sheepish when he contacted me mid-morning the day after the 1975 deer season had ended and said he had had a lion incident at his home.

Jim lives about nine miles north of Prescott in what was then a sparsely settled area populated by the horse-and-pickup set so common in Arizona towns. His property bordered a major paved county road and was surrounded on three sides by one- to five-acre parcels of land holding horses, humans, and myriads of free-ranging dogs. The land across the county road opens into unpopulated country which butts up, some two to three miles distant, against Granite Mountain—a known lair of lions.

The previous evening, a California hunter befriended by Jim had parked his Airstream trailer and International Travelall on Jim's land in a flat area near the county road. The hunter had been successful and had tied his quartered deer, well wrapped in canvas, on top of his Travelall. He opened the canvas at dark to allow the meat to chill overnight, in preparation for the drive across the desert to San Diego on the following day. The Travelall was unhitched from the trailer and parked alongside. The hunter slept inside his trailer with windows open, ten feet or less from his parked vehicle.

When he awoke at dawn and went out to cover his meat before the sun could warm it, he found two quarters missing. Suspecting dogs, he searched the immediate vicinity and found one quarter, relatively undamaged, lying alongside the road. The second quarter was never found. Large, dog-sized tracks were apparent in the dust on the hood of his vehicle and in the dirt surrounding it. The hunter was still cursing the neighborhood dogs when he brought Higgs down to view the situation. Jim immediately identified the tracks as those of a lion.

An early morning trial in town kept Jim from contacting me right away. By the time I arrived, the Travelall, trailer, and deer remains were en route to California. Horses, dogs, and people had trampled the area where the vehicle had been parked. We took hounds across the road to get a verification of the track and, perhaps, to view the lion if it had bedded nearby.

Chink, Moonshine, and Rattler immediately opened and left the area at a run. They trailed rapidly for about a mile to the base of Granite Mountain, then lost the track. We never found the second quarter of deer meat and do not know whether the lion was hidden in a deep recess amidst the boulders or had totally left the area. Though I never saw the track, I do not doubt Jim's identification. It was seconded by my strike dog, Chink.

As mentioned in earlier chapters, when instances such as this occur, the offending animal routinely turns out to be a young cat—in the early transient category, perhaps one-and-a-half to two-and-a-half years of age. I was once called to investigate reports of a lion stealing chickens and ducks in the mining-town-

89

turned-art-community of Jerome, Arizona. We did not see the cat, and it ultimately ceased to raid the chicken coops. Tracks in the area, however, identified it as a young lion out on its own.

An abundance of such exceptions to the norm in lion-killing behavior could be cited, but they are the exceptions. In most cases, lions follow a fairly uniform pattern in killing behavior, prey selection, and prey use. Understanding these behavior patterns is essential to understanding and accepting truth regarding lions.

Few people have seen lions make kills in the wild. Considerable myth surrounds the way it is done. While there are many ways prey can be approached, I suspect it is usually done, insofar as possible, in a fairly consistent manner. I also suspect that the techniques involved are very similar to those used by house cats, for which there is no shortage of observations.

Animal behaviorists have observed house-cat attacks closely and frequently. Their work provides a scenario that at least generally seems to coincide with observations of sign around lion kills. First and foremost, with the exception of the cheetah, cats are stalkers, not chasers. They attempt to stay invisible, either by way of ambush or, more often, stealth, until close enough to prey to attack. "Close enough" for lions, where wild prey such as deer are involved is probably fifty feet or less. They must make a dash, catch the prey unawares, and dispatch it before it can reach escape speed. Lions can seldom outrun their prey, and they have no stamina for long chases. They must strike quietly and quickly. And they must kill efficiently.

Solitary predators such as the lion cannot afford killing procedures which involve actual combat with prey. They depend heavily on efficient functioning of their bodies as killing machines. Too great a risk of injury would ultimately lead to death, if not from the injury itself, then to starvation due to debility. Again, lions must kill efficiently and well. And sign around kills suggests they do. Most kills made by mature, experienced lions, show little sign of struggle on the part of the prey animal.

Behaviorists' observations of house cats suggest an almost mechanical, instinctive approach to killing designed for prey within a particular size range. The classical kill is made with a stealthy approach, a short dash with belly to the ground, an attack which involves rising on the hind legs and planting the claws of a fore paw in the shoulder or flank of the prey. The lion must be able to reach over the animal's back, preferably with hind feet planted. This gives strength and stability to the attack and forces the prey off its feet virtually on the spot. Such a scenario is in contrast to the myth of lions dashing and jumping onto the backs of animals or jumping on prey from trees or ledges. Again, efficiency and avoidance of injury demand an approach which minimizes danger to the predator. A wild ride through low-hanging trees on the back of a deer or elk would be much too risky.

Once the claws are hooked, the lion's jaws and teeth come into play. If the height of the prey is the first size limitation involved in its selection—ideally it must be low enough for the lion to rear and reach over its back without totally leaving the ground—the length and thickness of neck are also a limitation. The location of the initial bite is keyed in distance and perhaps angle to the point where the fore paw is anchored in the prey's shoulder. This is essentially determined by the lion's own anatomy. He can only reach so far. If the prey is anatomically suitable, as are deer, the lion's initial bite will penetrate slender neck muscles near the back of the skull and will contact the upper vertebrae of the neck. At this point, sensitive nerve endings at the base of the lion's teeth tell it when the canines are aligned with gaps between the vertebrae, and the killing bite is swift and efficient. On larger animals, the lion may go for the throat rather than the vertebrae and resort to suffocation. This, however, entails more risk than the quick death by broken neck.

Keep in mind that this is probably the ideal scenario. Variation in prey size, lion size, angle of attack, and other circumstances undoubtedly make most killing situations less than perfect, but this seems, mechanically, to be the process for which the lion is adapted. If it has to deviate from this pattern very often, due to low densities of acceptable prey or inadequate stalking habitat, it will be at an increasing disadvantage. Risks will increase, and chances of survival will decline. Like all of us, the lion must play the odds.

Evidence, again from domestic cats, suggests that eating does not always begin immediately after the prey is down. Seemingly the excitement and exercise of the kill leave the digestive system unprepared for immediate intake. The cat may rest an hour or more before starting its meal. At some point, it will usually carry or drag the carcass to a protected spot, normally under a low-hanging tree, to do its feeding.

Before opening the carcass, lions remove hair around the point of incision with their incisors. The area around the entry point is bared much like an area prepared for surgery. The advantages of this for keeping meat hair free are obvious. Entry is usually made through the flank, just behind the ribs. I suspect it's done with claws, but I'm not sure. Both teeth and claws may be used.

Once the carcass is opened, the paunch and intestines are pulled out and away from the edible parts. These are usually found at the site of the first burial of the kill. Lungs, liver, and heart are apparently eaten early; the rib cage is chewed away to reach these. Seemingly the rear quarters most often get next attention, with the meat on the inside of the legs being eaten before meat on the outside. The cats seem to go first for the parts that will cool most slowly. They are also the parts that can be eaten with minimum exposure of meat to debris when the carcass is covered.

If the initial feeding follows a relatively long fast, it will be probably be large. Eight to ten pounds of meat may be engorged. The carcass is then covered and the cat retreats to a suitable spot, usually very close to the kill, to rest.

Period of use of a kill varies with size of lion, size of prey, and weather conditions. One of Hornocker's associates in Idaho, John Seidensticker, noted an instance where a lion stayed with an elk carcass for nineteen days during a cold period. We seldom saw use of a carcass for over four days in Arizona, with two or three being more common. Our warm midday temperatures taint kills rapidly.

There often seems to be a surprising amount of movement around kills, as if the lion is restless but doesn't want to risk leaving the site. If the cat has bedded some distance from the kill, say a quarter of a mile or more, a virtual lion path will develop between kill and bed sites over a two or three day period. The lion either feeds upon or checks the kill at fairly short intervals. The relatively low frequencies of reuse and reburial of kills suggests that most of these visits are security checks rather than feeding trips.

Kills are rarely fed upon more than once per day. Feeding requires dragging the carcass out of its burial site, and moving it far enough to shake off dirt and debris. Obviously, this process does not lend itself to multiple feedings through the day.

A kill is usually buried at the site of the first feeding. The cat stands over the kill and drags material inward with its front feet. Pine needles, limbs, and small twigs will be used. Even soil and small rocks will be used if nothing else is available. One of our radioed females, finding no other material in a granite boulder pile, carefully placed a single twig atop a dead mule deer buck before leaving. Kills are normally buried in a shady spot. Burial helps hide them from scavengers, such as coyotes and ravens, and it undoubtedly serves as insulation to keep the meat cool and fresh.

Exactly what causes ultimate abandonment of a kill is not known. Some are left after one feeding with much meat uneaten. Others are cleaned up completely, even the bone marrow being consumed. Taste of the individual prey animal and ambient temperature, hence rate of spoilage, may bring about kill abandonment. Disturbances at the kill site may have an effect also.

The most complete consumption of prey is usually accomplished by a female with advanced young. The disheveled appearance of kill sites with this class of lions present has been mentioned in an earlier chapter. Once seen, it is easy to recognize.

Females with young are also the most frequent killers. Maintaining a litter of large kittens requires a lot of meat. I've visited several sites where two or even three carcasses were present within a hundred-yard radius. These have either been all deer or combinations of deer and calves. Such killing behavior is an extremely efficient manner for a female to feed young. It may also represent periods of training, or practice, where advanced young are present and doing some of the actual killing. Quite often, if does with fawns are taken, the carcass of the fawn will also be found nearby. They apparently hang around after the mother is killed. Killing a doe with a fawn may offer the young lions low-risk opportunities to practice their predation skills.

The above activities around kills leave distinct sign that identify a given carcass as a lion kill. If the kill is fresh enough, tooth marks on the neck or throat and the distance between these marks help identify the predator. The method of entering the carcass, mentioned above, is also distinctive for lions. Drag marks between burial sites and the burial sites themselves are all characteristic of lions. And, of the course, there are the tracks of the animal. These characteristics, though seemingly subtle to the untrained, take on the aspect of neon lights advertising "lion kill" to those who view them frequently.

CHAPTER TWELVE
Predation

 No doubt exists that lions kill a variety of prey. What this does to the numbers of prey and what significance it has to humans, especially ranchers and deer hunters, is not easily unraveled.

Approximately 30 percent of the diet of lions living on the Spider-Cross U study area was made up of beef. Lions preferred calves, killed a few yearlings, and rarely took a mature cow. No evidence of lions eating mature bulls was found. Extrapolation of these figures led to estimates of a potential of a hundred head of cattle per year (mainly calves) being taken by lions from the two ranches during the study period. These two ranches ran a total of about 900 cows on approximately 175 square miles. Monetary loss involved would, of course, depend upon the current state of inflation, but a potential of $20,000 to $25,000 per year for the combined ranches was a conservative estimate. Thus for the Spider and Cross U ranches, the problem with lions was real.

It should be noted that the deer herd was at a relative low during the five years we spent at Spider-Cross U. Thus cattle losses may have been higher than under conditions of higher deer numbers. One of the complicating factors in lion-cattle predation lies in the fact that the calf crop hits its peak in late winter and early spring. This is the period when the deer herd is at its annual low. In pre-livestock times, the lion population would have declined when the deer population reached a critical low. Under present conditions, the presence of an abundance of calves, exactly at the time of year a lion population would normally have been stressed, serves to prop up lion numbers in the face of low native prey numbers.

This may serve to hold deer numbers down, as well as livestock. Our data from both the Kaibab and the Spider Ranch indicated that lions prefered deer over cattle on a ratio of about 3:2, if relative abundance of the two prey species was taken into consideration. Lions would therefore continue to select deer over cattle even when deer numbers were low, but the presence of calves at the critical period would allow lions to survive. Since cattle numbers are sustained at the allotment level by the rancher, the net results could be long-termed depression of deer numbers and continued heavy predation on calves. As in most ecological matters, the best conclusion to be drawn from all of this is that things are never as simple as they seem.

To date, few other studies have been published regarding the impact of lions on domestic prey species. At a gathering of lion specialists in Reno in 1976, livestock depredations were discussed in some detail. While the real situation must await reporting of data from all areas, a pattern of sorts did seem to evolve from this discussion.

Insofar as cattle losses in the United States are concerned, the southwestern states have the only problems of magnitude. Arizona consistently reports the greatest losses, followed by New Mexico, and perhaps, California. Losses of cattle further north seem to be relatively low. Sheep losses, on the other hand, occur throughout the western states. They are usually localized, but a sizeable amount of damage can occur in a short time. Solitary lions have been known to kill twenty sheep or more on bed grounds in one night. This can happen several nights in a row unless the lion involved is killed or the sheep moved a long distance.

In our Arizona study area, essentially all lions were taking beef at least part of the time. Thus the concept of good versus bad lions, stock killers versus nonstock killers, did not hold. In the case of localized sheep depredations, single lions are often involved, and the removal of an individual may solve the problem for a year or so.

Recent work by biologists has left some uncertainty regarding the real effect of lions on deer populations. In the Idaho study, Hornocker was able to conclude that lions were not preventing the deer population from increasing. The big game range in that primitive area was actually slightly overstocked, by his estimation. On the Spider-Cross U in Arizona, we concluded that lions alone would not prevent the deer population from increasing. They were, however, the single largest source of mule deer mortality on the area, and lion predation, along with losses to coyotes, disease, sport hunting, and poaching, was keeping the herd at a relatively low level.

It would appear that, in this situation, removal of a large number of lions from the area would stimulate the deer herd. In reality, things were not so clear-cut. The area was reopened to lion hunting in 1976, after five years of closure. Average annual kill for the next five years on the Spider ranch was ten lions per year. This came from an area of about 175 square miles. By 1986 the deer herd had increased, but not markedly. Deer populations in similar habitat throughout the state had also increased.

For some reason, the Kaibab gave an opposite picture. We started work on lions there in 1977, after the deer population had been declining for some ten years. Our initial estimate of lion numbers, approximately forty resident adults, suggested that lions might be numerous enough to account for the losses of deer that couldn't be attributed to hunting or other causes. In 1978, the lion population declined to an estimated fifteen resident adults. This was due in part to a relatively heavy take by sport hunters and probably even more to heavy natural mortality resulting from a low deer population and the extremely severe 1977-78 winter. The Kaibab deer herd immediately began a recovery and has continued to increase. Other things were happening on the Kaibab during this time, including some exceptionally wet years that may have also stimulated the deer population. Nonetheless, we cannot ignore the fact that the deer population turned up just at the time that the lion population hit a low. The whole scenario, viewing all of the various studies, suggests that we still do not understand clearly the factors affecting either predator or prey numbers and that results from one area may have little or no predictive value in another.

As a result of the above incongruities, controversies will continue regarding how humans should deal with lions. Control will still be a recommended option, at least for a while. Three tools, historically, have been used to control lions: hunting with dogs, trapping, and poison. I will deal with the latter first, because it is probably a vestige of past wildlife management technology. I find it hard to believe that the public in general will ever tolerate extended poisoning operations for any wildlife again, regardless of its economic benefits.

Since lions tend to feed upon animals they have killed themselves, use of poisoned baits is probably not an effective means of lion control anyway. Coyotes and foxes are normally relatively abundant in lion country, and these canids are much more likely to find baits and consume them than are lions. Poisoning of carcasses of lion-killed prey can perhaps be effective. However, as discussed earlier, finding a large number of lion kills without the help of dogs or radioed lions is unlikely. Hence, while a few animals might be killed with poisoned carcasses, heavy impact on a large lion population will probably not happen using this technique. If it would, previous attempts to eliminate lions in this manner would probably have already succeeded.

The tendency for young lions—the so-called transients—to take unusual prey or foods might make them susceptible to poison. Such animals could well feed upon freshly-killed and poisoned carcasses. A program using 1080 or strychnine in large portions of meat, horse quarters for example, placed strategically in lion country and frequently replenished could impact these younger classes. This would ultimately affect the overall lion population by eliminating recruitment. Because of the transient nature of young lions, however, such a program would have to be carried out for several years and would have to cover all of the lion country in a state to be effective. It would need to be repeated at least three out of every ten years. Impact on non-target animals would be severe, and the expense of such an operation boggles the mind. Political and logistical difficulties are even more mind-boggling. I doubt that it will happen.

Another method of lion control is trapping. This can be effective in limited areas, for lions are not difficult to catch in steel traps. They do not come to scent baits well, however, and blind sets in canyon bottoms or along rims seem to work best. I've heard that some trappers use catnip to good advantage. Probably the greatest limitation to trapping lions is the amount of time and labor involved in making and maintaining adequate sets. The expense of large traps in the first place and the infrequency with which a lion may pass a particular place make lion trapping a difficult and costly operation. And, as with poison, it must be maintained constantly for an extended period of time over a large area. Time, trouble, and expense all rule against this technique for long-term population control.

Finally comes hunting with dogs. As we've already seen, it is by far the most entertaining means of taking lions, but it requires considerable time and skill. It suffers from the same difficulties as other methods in that it must be constantly maintained over large areas to achieve its purpose. Hunting with dogs is productive as a means of guiding sport hunters; it probably has little real use in lion control.

Actually, the information available on lion population biology suggests strongly that control of lions is unlikely to occur and is definitely not cost-efficient. In the Idaho primitive area, where no control occurred, no livestock existed, and natural prey was extremely abundant, lions built to a stable population density, established home areas, and did not increase beyond that point. That density was about one lion per sixteen square miles of habitat on the winter range. It was lower in the summer because the cats spread over the larger summer range.

On the Spider-Cross U study area in Arizona, where lions used the same habitats year-round, and no strong seasonal climatic constraints existed, the population seemingly leveled off at about one adult lion per eighteen square miles of habitat. On the Kaibab, we found similar peak densities before the decline, if lions on winter range or summer range were considered separately. In all studies of lions where relatively good documentation of lion numbers has been made, lion densities have peaked and stabilized at points between ten and twenty square miles per adult resident. Evidence indicates that, if left alone, adult resident lions will probably not populate beyond such densities.

We hear rumors of exceptions to such numbers, but to date the exceptions all involve removal of apparently large numbers of lions from limited areas. The high removal of lions during the first five years that the Spider Ranch was opened to hunting is an example. That such a phenomenon is possible seems to be explained by the behavior of the transient segment of lion populations. Stability of lion numbers in a given area is apparently maintained by the established adult resident lions. The exact mechanism used to prevent new lions from establishing in a saturated area is unknown, but all scientific evidence to date suggests it occurs. One study of a hunted population in Idaho suggests that this same saturation density applies even where resident lions are being removed.

Movement of transients into an area, however, apparently occurs rapidly when removal of lions begins. If adequate lion habitat surrounds an area undergoing intensive control, replacement will probably at least equal removal. Some workers have even suggested that removal of residents from such a limited area would increase lion densities because two or more transients might temporarily vie for a gap created by removal of a single established resident.

To provide an example, let's imagine a ranch of about 350 square miles in an area where lion control is to be applied. Saturation population, using one resident lion per 17.5 square miles, would be about twenty adult lions for the entire ranch. Kittens and transients moving through will add to this figure. Let's assume that this ranch is surrounded by an additional 3500 square miles of equally good lion habitat, supporting two hundred additional adult resident lions. Our data from the Spider ranch suggested a male:female ratio of 2:3, hence eight of the adults on the ranch would be males; twelve would be females. On the surrounding area an additional 80 males and 120 females would make up the breeding population.

Data gathered to date suggest that about two kittens survive to transient age out of every litter produced by an adult female and that each female produces about one litter every other year. This being the case, female mountain lions replace themselves approximately every year, hence the ranch would produce about twelve new lions per year; the surrounding country an additional

120. Presumably, the rancher would have to kill twelve lions per year to break even.

This, however, would buy him nothing; it would merely hold the population about where it would have stayed if left alone. Even if the rancher were able to remove twenty to thirty lions per year from his ranch, he probably would see no real change, because the surrounding country would provide more than enough to replace his kill. We do not know what the natural mortality is for adult residents under unstressed conditions, but it seems to be relatively low. Hornocker noted only one to two adults lost over eight years in his Idaho study area. Hence, something on the order of 100 to 120 lions per year would have to be removed from the vicinity of our hypothetical ranch for a period of several years before any real change in lion numbers might be seen. From such data, it seems that, in good lion habitat, attempts to control lions at any feasible level will probaby accomplish nothing.

As mentioned above, actual events on the Spider-Cross U area seem to support this idea. The area was closed to lion hunting from fall 1971, to early summer 1976. A few lions were killed on surrounding, unclosed, areas during this period, but the closure was basically effective. During the winter of 1976-77, after the closure was lifted, thirteen lions were taken. The mean estimated density for the previous three years was ten adult resident lions. During the second winter after the closure, bad weather kept hunters out. Only two lions were taken. During the third winter (1978-79), fifteen lions were killed in the area, and ten were killed in 1979-80. At present, lion densities in the area seem as high as ever, and the ranch owner says his calf crops have not increased. Events on the Kaibab from 1977 to 1980 suggest that it is more isolated from other areas of good lion habitat, and when its population declines, replacement occurs much more slowly. This may explain why lion control has appeared to be so effective in stimulating the Kaibab deer herd in the past. (Interestingly enough, the Kaibab has been the example used to demonstrate both the effectiveness and the dangers of predator control. The Kaibab may be, by its very isolated nature, a unique situation.)

An obvious question arising from this analysis is: what happens to the transients when a population isn't controlled? This is not known, but we have some ideas from limited observations. For one thing, based upon the Idaho data and limited data from the Kaibab, we know that some young transient lions will travel a long distance, perhaps seventy-five to one hundred miles from their mother's home area upon dispersal. Recently, a lion marked as a juvenile in the Bighorn Mountains of Wyoming turned up in northern Colorado, 350 airline miles from where it was marked.

These transients may wander for a year or more before settling down. Some of these dispersing young will find areas vacated by older lions who have died or are old enough to be displaced. The remainder of these transient young, along with the displaced aged, are probably forced into poor environments, away from good prey habitat, and perhaps into areas where chances of contact with humans are increased. Those that contact humans are likely to get into trouble. Such are the lions that kill chickens in Jerome, steal deer in Prescott's outskirts, attack poodles in Scottsdale, or lead Tucson city police on wild chases.

In fact, recent events in California suggest that this problem of transient lions may be the best justification for continued sporting harvest, or in some cases, moderate rates of control in wild lion populations. California, due entirely to political pressure by animal protection groups, has allowed no lion hunting for sixteen years. Unusual events between humans and lions seem to have increased. This has culminated in two recent attacks by young lions on children in a state park. Although California is not the only state that has experienced attacks by lions on humans during the past decade, the families of the children sued the state and county for $50 million for mismanagement of the lion and failure to take proper safety precautions for the public.

Large urban areas butting up against wild expanses of potential lion habitat are a fairly common reality in the West. Presence of humans on wildlands is equally real. Encounters between humans and lions are inevitable and are normally without serious consequence. Where lions are totally protected for extended periods, however, undesirable incidences, caused by the influx of inexperienced transients into urban areas, are likely to increase. The ultimate result of this is bad press for the lion. If moderate rates of harvest reduce these incidences by keeping territories open in the wilds, then sport hunting of lions may help to guarantee the species' continued existence.

On a planet where human flesh constitutes such a high percentage of the biomass and where all wild things seem forced to compete economically for the land, total protection of a species may not work to its benefit in the long run. Yet many people would still eliminate hunting of lions, as well as other species, feeling that only complete protection can save these species from extinction.

CHAPTER THIRTEEN
Extinction, Natural Balance, Sanitation

 Studies of the mountain lion over the past twenty years have tended to diffuse any claims that the species is endangered by extinction in the western United States, western Canada, and most of Latin America. As a species, it seems to be secure. However, the eastern subspecies of lion is apparently extirpated, and the Florida subspecies is definitely endangered. At least one subspecies of Arizona lion may have quietly gone extinct while no one was looking—if it ever existed to begin with. The whole notion of endangered subspecies and the fact that they have been given legal recognition in the Endangered Species Laws, creates special problems for the field biologist. To understand this, one must understand what constitutes a subspecies.

The specialized portion of biology that spends its time identifying and describing species is called taxonomy. For early field biologists, it was the vogue to identify a new species and have your name attached to it in one way or the other. Modern taxonomy is based upon the the binomial nomenclature system devised by Linnaeus in the sixteenth century. Since this basic approach to classifying animals originated, many thousands of naturalists have spent their time finding new biological entities to name. Their specialty constituted one of the major forms of activity in biology until early in this century. It is less in vogue now, because we have run out of geographic frontiers to explore. Unidentified species still exist, but they are increasingly difficult to find. The field of taxonomy has reached the point of diminishing returns. Only the very specialized and very determined are still looking.

Taxonomists, historically, are an interesting group of people. Probably no segment of early scholarly endeavor had a larger group of egoists rushing to have their name in the annals of science. Organisms were named and renamed in many parts of the world, and arguments over priority, dates, and so on, prevailed to the point of chaos. The accepted names of some species are still being challenged as modern taxonomic scholars sift the literature and uncover obscure "priors" that invalidate long-used and accepted scientific names. (In fact, it appears that Puma might ultimately be accepted over Felis for the generic name of the mountain lion.)

Taxonomists dealing with many lower organisms such as insects have even had difficulty in defining species, but in the wild mammals, the term probably needs no sophisticated definition. Creatures that look alike, behave alike, and interbreed are usually designated as distinct. Thus African lions are a species, tigers are a species, and mountain lions are a species.

By the time new species had begun to run low, however, taxonomists had discovered variation within species, especially those with wide geographical distribution. Fights and confusion broke out when they tried to break these down into new species, and it was here that the subspecies, or race, classification originated. This is a functional classification that allows working biologists to acknowledge regional variations within species. It has ecological significance and relates to habitat. However, as in many cases where egoistic human endeavor is involved, early workers were perhaps overzealous or at least premature in some of their classifications.

Taxonomy has been plagued throughout its history by a rift between two basic philosophies—the lumpers and the splitters. The first of these tends to recognize as few categories as possible; the second tends to proliferate names of species or subspecies on basis of minute variations in animal populations. Both schools of thought have some merit in application, but, obviously, the splitters have included among their ranks some very ambitious people. A classic example is the case of C. Hart Merriam, a man famous in the field of plant ecology for his recognition of life zones. Using mainly skull measurements from museum specimens, he classified seventy-eight species of bears in the United States. We now know that bears are highly variable, that color variations can occur even within litters, that color changes with age in individuals, and that skull characteristics vary greatly. Bears, excluding polar bears, fall into two species in the United States: black bears and brown (or grizzly) bears.

Ferreting out indiscrete classifications and putting them into more functional form has occupied the careers of many modern biologists. The job is not complete, and many questionable subspecies are still recognized in the literature. Until recently, this was of little consequence to anyone. Individuals working closely with a given species knew it well enough to recognize where valid and invalid classifications existed. They simply shrugged off the invalid ones and chuckled at the personalities that created such confusion. Subspecific classifications, or ecotypes, were mainly used to delineate the geographical area where one was working.

With recent concern over extinctions, however, the whole tone of animal taxonomy has changed. The terms species and subspecies have taken on legal definitions. The federal Endangered Species Act, in fact, includes a "look-alike" clause which allows an entire species to be fully protected throughout its range, if only a small subspecies within some obscure part of its range can be called endangered. To date, this clause has not been applied unreasonably, but it has wild and woolly possibilities with regard to the lion.

At present, thirty subspecies of mountain lions are recognized in the taxonomic literature. As already mentioned, the Florida lion is classified as endangered and is now fully protected. The eastern cougar subspecies, once occurring throughout states east of the Mississippi is considered extirpated, although people in the East continue to report sightings of cougars.

So far, the look-alike clause of the Endangered Species Act has not been invoked to protect the lion in the West. The remoteness of the Florida lion from the western lion, coupled, I suspect, with the difficulties involved in enforcing such a classification without cooperation, of the rural population in the large expanses of western lion habitat has suppressed such a move. Also, as mentioned earlier, recent studies have confirmed the health of lion populations in most western states. There are sub-species in the West, however, that might be considered endangered.

The Colorado Desert lion, better known as the Yuma Puma, and the Baja California lions, for example, apparently exist in extremely low densities. Classification of these subspecies occurred about 1900 and was based upon small numbers of specimens. Only nine specimens were examined in the case of the Colorado Desert lion and two for the Baja lion. Both races border ranges of more abundant races and of each other. Suitable lion habitat along the Colorado has virtually disappeared as land has been developed for agriculture and recreation. Desert areas back from the river are rapidly being denuded by recreational vehicle enthusiasts and by masses of wintering retirees who camp, for free, in the desert. The last bastions of the Yuma Puma, if it ever existed, are probably the military gunnery ranges and the Cabeza Prieta Wildlife Refuge, where human entry is restricted. Deer and bighorn sheep densities in these areas, however, are so low that existence of a lion population is doubtful.

Whether these subspecies were ever valid is open to question. In a species such as the lion, where transient animals regularly travel fifty to one hundred miles in establishing new home areas, one wonders if racial classifications as these might not be eliminated with more information. Even the Florida race as it presently stands was classified on the basis of only seventeen museum specimens. It, too, historically bordered the ranges of other subspecies and thus may have merely been an extension of the eastern cougar.

Similarly, the Yuma Puma of Arizona may have been the same lion that exists throughout higher elevations in the central parts of the state. The desert habitat was simply less hospitable, hence lion densities remained low. These populations could have been made up entirely of animals that had not found suitable home areas in better habitat. Our laws regarding the management of the species are now influenced by such questionable classifications, which in the long run may slow reestablishment of species in historical range. Puritanically holding out for "eastern" cougar blood, for example, could prevent transplants of lions from other suitable habitats into historical eastern cougar range if it is available. We are, perhaps, being more puritanical than nature.

Because of the above uncertainties, the whole notion of subspecies in lions is now being reevaluated. A recent assessment of several original Yuma Puma specimens by a group of California biologists has reaffirmed the reality of hair and skull differences reported by early taxonomists. Recent examination of Florida panther specimens by a research veterinarian, on the other hand, has thrown doubt upon some of the key physical characteristics used to differentiate that race. The white hairs on the back, thought to be a phenotypic characteristic of the Florida subspecies, for example, may merely be hairs turned white by tick bites. Some of the other characteristics may be a result of inbreeding due to genetic isolation of the remnant population rather than racial characteristics resulting from evolutionary adaptations.

In conjunction with the Florida panther work, the National Institute of Health is now addressing mountain lion genetics using the most modern serological techniques, wherein the actual genetic diversity within a species can be viewed at the cellular level. These techniques, when applied to the cheetah in Africa, disclosed little variation for that species across the entire continent. Such new tools are rapidly revising the whole field of animal taxonomy and may modify our concept of extinct races drastically as their results become known.

Concerning the so-called balance of nature, I find myself tempted to write impatiently, "It doesn't exist." The concept of a stable, balanced planet, devoid of humans, where predators eat just enough prey to save the bushes, is such a severe oversimiplification of reality that all working biologists find it offensive. It seems to be a pseudoscientific extension of the notion of the garden of Eden. In reality, life on this planet has been dynamic and changing for millions of years, with species coming and going and with temporary balances being destroyed. Nothing ever stays the same, and for humans to believe that they can freeze the clock at some particular time, with regard to habitat and wild species compositions, is extremely naive. More and more, we realize that we work within the processes of change, and while our presence seems to have influenced their direction and rate, I'm not sure that we really have much to do with their control. We have, perhaps, oversold the idea of wildlife management.

The studies already mentioned to this point demonstrate the variability in lion-prey relations. In the Idaho Wilderness Area, for example, unregulated lion populations during the period of the study seemed to do little to control numbers of deer and elk. On the North Kaibab, lions may have been instrumental in depressing the mule deer herd during the early seventies. A sudden decline in lion numbers in 1978 certainly released the herd and allowed it to begin a rapid increase. At this point, we do not know for sure what caused the lions to decline. On the Spider-Cross U area, heavy removal of lions for five years between 1976 and 1981 apparently did not significantly reduce the lion population. The deer herd increased slowly during this period, as did deer herds in surrounding habitat where lions were not heavily hunted.

In all of these examples, we as biologists could see events within the populations, but were unable to explain exactly why different populations reacted in different ways. Thus broad generalizations regarding the balance of nature are very likely to leave us cold. More and more, we realize that nature is so complex that we must deal with specifics, monitoring events daily on the ground. We are a long way from understanding the causes of these events, but we must work with the hand we're dealt. To base our management (or lack of it) on an idealized era prior to the coming of the white man is unrealistic. It will simply lead to more confusion. In truth, we don't have that choice. Whatever our ideals, we have to make decisions and act in the here and now. In so doing, we are living as part of nature.

Sanitation is an idea that has elements of truth, but that has been distorted and oversimplified in application. It is a notion that biologists created, in essence an application of Darwin's theory of natural selection. As we understand the true complexities of wild populations, we are, to some extent having to live down such earlier, simplistic notions, that we have placed in the conventional wisdom. In sanitation, predators take only the weak, halt, and lame from a prey population, thus removing individuals incapable of surviving. When this notion is carried to extremes, it ceases to describe nature in reality. While predators may have selected against the less healthy or more stupid individuals in a prey population in the past, and they undoubtedly continue to do so, the phenomenon functions on a statistical level. Certainly the odds of an older, sicker, or dumber animal being taken by a predator may be high. Some aspects of lion behavior suggest, however, that they may actually tend to select for younger and more active animals—that lions are triggered to attack active prey. Nature does not necessariy comply with the rules that humans conceive, and the evolution of a predator designed to survive on healthy prey is certainly not impossible.

At any rate, the selection of incompetent individuals by predators, where it occurs, is a statistical matter, not a constant. Probably no predator eats only very sick or old prey. Certainly lions do not. In the long run, gleaning of weaker animals may occur, but at low prey densities with good habitat, such animals are very much in the minority. Predators would hardly survive under such circumstances.

Thus it seems that we have a way to go in understanding lions and their impacts on prey. Whatever our level of knowledge as biologists, the ultimate decisions regarding hunting of lions, hunting of prey, and use of the lands where lions and their prey live will be determined by political interaction of all humans—hunters, ranchers, preservationists, and biologists.

CHAPTER FOURTEEN
The Morals
of Management

 One of the principles of population genetics says that, granted no major environmental disturbance, the proportion of a particular gene, thus the particular physical manifestation of that gene, will stay relatively constant in an animal population. The proportion of people with brown and blue eyes in North America, for example, stays fairly constant from generation to generation, being determined by the frequency in human cells of those genes that determine these colors. As a biologist working with a controversial species, I've formed the notion that human beliefs, at least the proportions of different individuals that support a particular kind of belief, are also fairly constant through time. I have developed an uneasy feeling that the proportion of mystics, agnostics, and atheists; of power-seeking dominants and individualistic recluses; and of predator-haters and predator-lovers may all be determined by genetic or cultural inheritance. If this is true, no amount of new knowledge will rapidly change the emotional response, thus the manner of dealing with predators, by any individual group. We will always have a certain percentage of people with particular attitudes. The very fact that conservative religions have survived in the face of modern cosmology is compelling evidence that this thought is valid.

All human acts can be deemed detrimental to some other species. We, like all other life forms, are consumptive. Our presence, to some extent, undoubtedly prevents the existence of some other organism. The same is true of deer, cows, lions, or whatever. It cannot be otherwise. The fallacy in our thinking has always been our efforts to separate humankind from nature. This applies to utilitarian hunters and ranchers and to pure preservationists alike. In truth, we are part of the natural machine. We exist. We must understand our role and make our choices. And because we are so abundant, whether we like it, dislike it, or are totally apathetic to the idea, our choices will influence the lion.

Absolute moralistic opposition to killing of animals cannot be countered on an equally moral plain. A world in which no death occurred—and in which there was no atavistic joy in killing—might be a beautiful world. If it were available, even though I grew up a hunter, I would now probably choose it. In reality, however, we deal daily with the world that is. It includes death from a variety of causes. Whether humans hunt or not, death will occur in nature. As long as we do not drive other species to extinction, the morality of hunting must be up to the individual.

The economic contributions of hunters, via licenses and firearms taxes, to protection and management of wildlife has been adequately heralded. Game departments, wildlife research, and game wardens protecting all wildlife probably would not exist if it were not for formalized hunting and the revenue it provides. People killing wildlife would exist; legal hunters would not.

From a practical standpoint, hunters save wildlife. Be this as it may, the killing of an animal like a lion for sporting purposes is perhaps even more difficult to justify than controlling it for protection of livestock. Lion control for the benefit of the rancher at least claims to protect someone's livelihood and to lower costs of protein for human consumption.

Control of lions to produce more deer is even more difficult to justify than sport hunting of lions, for its aim is to save deer to be killed by people. The deer still die. If effective, such lion control might make sense economically, for more deer mean more deer hunters and this means more revenue for game and fish agencies. Theoretically this should benefit a broader base of wildlife, but it may be too coldly practical.

As is the case with most scientific data, the information we have regarding lions can be used to support the arguments on either side of the issue. All indications are that lions can sustain a fairly high rate of removal without permanently affecting their populations. That is to say, you really can't control them with practical levels of hunting or trapping. On one hand, hunting, or for that matter, control, does not hurt lion numbers, so must be OK. On the other hand, control is a serious waste of money, for it does no particular good. Choose your side and choose your argument. The lion as a species probably won't even notice.

Thus the current issue—to hunt or not to hunt—to control or not to control—is missing the point and accomplishing nothing. It is going nowhere because it is a meaningless issue. Those of us concerned with the lion need to look for more productive ground.

Since sport hunting does not seem to hurt the lion as a species, and since sport hunters provide funds for management of all species, sportsmen are off the environmental hook for now. Their decision is a moral one, and they have made it because they find hunting satisfying as a pursuit. This point of view cannot be attacked on a rational basis, and their activity makes the lion valuable to humans. The crux of the lion hunting issue lies between those who would intentionally reduce lion numbers, for deer or for cattle, and those who would totally protect them. The controllers seemingly have valid economic claims, at least in places; the protectors are certainly justified in placing their own, positive, value on the lion and requesting its continued existence. Neither side, however, seems to be seeking ways to accomplish their goals outside of the present narrow and polarized viewpoints. Nothing can change until both sides soften.

We have already seen that the absolute demand for control is somewhat impractical; it may not work. What are the problems of protectionism? If control is economically unfeasible, and if it does not work, should it not be opposed? I think lion control should stop, but, unless the species is truly endangered, control must stop with the cooperation of the rancher. Pressures to rapidly change traditional methods only create resistance and increase unlawful activity. In Arizona at present, for example, we have evidence that the unreported lion kill by ranchers equals at least 25 to 35 percent of the reported legal harvest. It may be much higher. Ranchers actually refuse to report lions they kill because of fear of increased regulation, even though the current law requires reporting of such lions taken. An increase in unenforceable laws would increase the cost of enforcement and decrease public compliance and public respect for all law. Laws or regulations in themselves do not solve a problem. This, I believe, is a lesson preservationists have not yet learned.

If we are to stop predator control (or lion control) completely, we must at the same time acknowledge the problems that lions cause ranchers on the land. I'm aware that an extremely good case can be made on broad economic grounds alone against the continued existence of range livestock on public lands in much of the West. Economic difficulties could eventually end the western range livestock industry. But this is none of my business. As a manager of wildlife, I must deal with what exists on the land. This includes cattle, sheep, and the people who own them. If we are to give the lion positive values and restrict the rancher's way of dealing with predation, we must also find ways to compensate him or help him solve his problem. Here, I think, is a practical place for protectionists to put their money.

I'm not necessarily suggesting that preservationists provide compensation to ranchers for losses. This could be unending and would probably be attended by all of the same problems of the bounty system, including fraud. This is not to suggest that ranchers are dishonest, but unethical people exist in all walks of life. Policing subsidies for livestock losses would be an expensive and difficult job. It might create more problems than it solved.

Far better would be money spent in attempting to develop better cattle, deer, ranch, and habitat management to alleviate losses. Research on lions to date has pointed up a variety of possible approaches to reducing cattle losses without lion control. There is an increasing need to try these ideas in a controlled situation, with cooperation and support of all groups interested in the lion.

My final thought, then, regarding political and regulatory activities of both ranchers and preservationists is that the time is right to contribute to programs seeking new solutions to problems. We need more adequate monitoring of individual circumstances rather than absolute regulations that fail to acknowledge the variations in nature's theme. Too often such regulations become symbols of political battles won, but nothing changes in reality on the ground. Problems are not solved, and species not necessarily saved.

The hunter has funded wildlife research for almost fifty years. He has, perhaps, a valid claim for preference in policies of game management. It is time for those who question hunting and for those who compete with it to provide a similar source of funds and information. Until they do, they will find resistance to their complaints, and they are fifty years behind.

Historically, we have looked to those we called leaders for wisdom in managing natural resources. Presumably, those that ascend in our system are the visionaries. Perhaps our expectations of them are too high. Whatever the case, it is the politicians, administrators, and the agencies they control that we must look to as we begin to consider our future concept of cougar.

SECTION FOUR

THE FUTURE

CHAPTER FIFTEEN
Administration

 Although this chapter is not at the end of the book, it was the last to be written. I avoided it for a long time, because it discloses negative attitudes that I have developed while working on lions. It can be construed as an attack on the system that has supported me for twenty-five years. Such is not my intent. The stories that follow are told to explain my own feelings as portrayed in the remainder of the book. And feelings are the the final products of such an intense experience as research on the lion.

Germane to my discussion in the previous chapter regarding relative proportions of different types of people in human populations, I've concluded after nearly twenty-five years in government that administrators and researchers will never quite get along. Their values are different, and they see the world, actually, the universe, from totally different perspectives. Over the years, I've developed the research perspective to what I suspect is an extreme. Others in research may not agree with me. Nonetheless, I have to express it here in order to clarify my attitude toward administrators, politicians, and agencies.

To do any sort of research using modern technology, money is needed. Hence a researcher must work for some large organization or must sell the idea of research on a subject to someone controlling money. This entails dealing with administrators and forces the researcher into a form of personal prostitution called justification. Justification is the process of telling administrators what value a particular piece of research has for the organization, its constituency, or the wildlife resource. Usually the value of research to the resource is a lesser consideration. In justifying research, value to humans is the main concern.

For the researcher, justification is not too difficult if the project involved is one that the scientist himself has discovered and designed. It is most difficult when the project is assigned by administration. A strange game often develops here where the scientist is handed a proposal for a project that is needed to solve some immediate problem, usually a controversial problem. Normally, the scientist is given a general statement of the information needed and asked to design and justify the project so that it can be funded. At this stage, a strange transition often takes place wherein the administrators disclaim the study and become a part of the power structure questioning the project's value. The researcher is forced to pretend that the project is his and defend it in front of the very people who came up with the idea in the first place. This process does not engender respect for administrations.

What's worse, almost invariably, once the project is justified, the researcher goes afield and spends three, five, or ten years of his or her professional life attempting to solve the problem. More often than not, by the time the results are in, the issue that created the study has long since passed, a new administration is in power, the scientist is criticized for wasting time on useless information, and handed another current problem to solve. In this process, administrators gain the advantage of being able to put off decisions on unpopular issues while appearing to be doing something. Researchers gain funding for research.

In the midst of it all, we sometimes improve our knowledge of nature, and to me that's what it's all about. This is the point at which I become a bit of an extremist, I think. As modern cosmological research progresses, we become more and more aware of the relative insignificance of our planet in the universe. We are a tiny planet in a relatively small galaxy that is one of billions. Our uniqueness is life. At this point we don't know if it exists anywhere else. Our species' uniqueness lies in our waxing awareness of our planet's uniqueness. Yet most of our day-to-day goals as individuals are centered around survival and personal gain, for ourselves and for subgroups of our species. Thus in wildlife agencies we justify our activities on the basis of producing more game for the hunter or on producing watchable wildlife for the nonhunter. Everything we do, to satisfy the political mind, must be justified by its value to humans.

Yet if we are nothing but a tiny planet in a nearly infinite universe, the cycle of living, surviving, acquiring, and dying becomes meaningless unless we add something while we're here. To date, the only growing entities that the human species has been able to add are technological capability and knowledge. In truth, we seem unable to keep ourselves from adding these, even in the face of power structures uneasy about new ideas. If this is all true, then, while we play the game of justifying research to foster the goals of an organization or an agency, to give more to the hunter or some other group, or, for that matter, to save another species, the ultimate value is the knowledge itself. The extent to which we gather knowledge and protect it for future generations, or perhaps for cultures from other worlds, is the extent to which we succeed as a species. Application of the knowledge and the selfish individual goals thus attained are just part of the process.

We may say we exist as researchers to benefit those that support us, but down deep we know we lie. In truth we believe that the organizations ultimately sell goods and services to provide a tiny profit that we use to further knowledge. In my mind, the only profit the human species creates in the frenzy of survival and acquisition is new knowledge. What I'm saying, I guess, is that, although I play the game of seeking knowledge to further the goals of Arizona Game and Fish Department, down deep I believe that the most important purpose of the department is to support my research. So I study lions and whatever else seems critical at the moment.

I first read Farley Mowat's *Never Cry Wolf* at about the time I was finishing my M.S. degree in wildlife management at the University of Idaho. I found his opening chapters, those dealing with the absurdities of logistics imposed upon him by the bureaucracy, hilarious beyond belief. These chapters highlighted the book, and I'm sure, entertained thousands of private citizens who assumed he was exaggerating. I read those chapters again after twenty-five years of employment with a government agency, and I shook my head in sad affirmation. The humor for me was gone.

For studying lions, like studying wolves, is an arduous task if you do it well. It cannot be done halfway. It is an all-or-none occupation, and it forces you into a realm that is alien to the workaday world of city humans. The very fact of entering this realm sets into motion a mental process that inevitably results in rejection and loss of faith in human agencies. The dilemma here, of course, is the knowledge that these very systems are providing the financial mechanism that allows you to continue to work. The resulting internal conflict can't be solved unless you become independently wealthy.

The deterioration of faith in leadership comes in pieces. Most incidents are insignificant in and of themselves. Additively, they can become unbearable. Perhaps a couple of stories—extremes cases, I'll admit—will help convey the feelings. We spent two winters at an Arizona Game and Fish Department installation on the North Kaibab called Ryan Station. "We" included myself and Priscilla, my wife at the time, Bill Powers and Linda, his wife at the time, and after Bill transferred, Norris Dodd and his wife at the time. Ryan is an idyllic installation at 6500 feet on the northwest corner of the Kaibab Plateau. It was perfect as a field station for research, given a modicum of support and permanency. The winters (1977-1979) that we occupied Ryan, however, included two of the wettest on record. Rain, interspersed with warm snow, fell almost daily during the first year. The winter range where we tried to mark lions became a morass of mud. Our study was budgeted for three years and not likely to be extended, so to succeed, we had to work regardless of conditions. We weren't inclined to blame weather for failure, and we felt that our work was important. It was, at least, important to us.

Snow fell almost daily during the second winter and piled three feet deep in our front yard at Ryan. Getting out of the yard was a major task at times; moving around the study area involved a four-wheel-drive vehicle with chains on all four tires. We spent as much time stuck as we did moving. Horses became unusable, and their care in the thigh-deep snow became a major effort in itself. Merely keeping water lines unfrozen took hours from each month. But we were still able to mark and study lions.

Again, success of the study for its own sake was important to us. It had nothing to do with the opinions of administrators

Day-to-day living at Ryan took a lot of time and energy. Cutting wood, hauling hay for horses, keeping water lines unfrozen, and more troublesome, free from airlocks in the faulty system that the department had installed twenty years earlier, were full-time jobs exclusive of research. The wives, isolated from society and finding no real identity for themselves in studying lions, became restless and disillusioned. (In fact, all three marriages ended shortly after the study was over.) But the time constraints of the project forced us to give these other problems as little attention as possible and to focus on marking and following lions. Who can say if it was worth it?

During the second winter, at each new snow, we drove the roads—all of them that we hoped to use. We had to keep them open. Timing was critical. If we waited too long, a chunk of country was closed off, inaccessible for work. The study suffered.

We spent days waiting for the right conditions to hunt. We also spent days stuck in axle-deep mud, digging out, walking out, sensing the weather, sensing the condition of the land, trying to accomplish just a little more. We were adequately outfitted for the field, so the circumstances were usually not life-threatening. They simply demanded immense amounts of energy for each small task accomplished. It was exhilarating and exhausting work; it destroyed other aspects of life.

We rode when we could. We herded hounds. We hunted hounds. We worried about lost hounds being caught in fur trappers' traps. The loss of one or two key dogs could make or break the study. Each judgement regarding travel over a certain road or area to hunt was a fine-line call that could affect the success of a day's work or the entire project itself. Hence, when we asked for assistance from those who paid our checks, we hoped they would seek ways to ease the job. Instead, too often, we encountered policies or high-level decisions that merely added to the energy drain and frustration.

A sense of betrayal from above set in. The water system went unfixed, though requests were made time after time—each time after we had dug through two feet of snow and three feet of mud to bare the pipes and pump them free of airlocks. The water tanks themselves had never been cleaned over the twenty-odd years they had functioned. We ultimately had to write hostile memos to get the tanks opened with acetylene torches for cleaning, and we did the cleaning. We found ample evidence of rodent remains in the water we had been drinking.

The problems would have all been bearable with a longer, more leisurely time to work and with the administrative backing, or with the freedom on our part to solve them. But the agency owned the land and the house, and the powers in Phoenix reserved the right to judge what was important. Our immediate supervisors tried to help, but each request for labor, funds, or equipment disappeared into a hierarchy that was at least six levels deep. The few decisions that came back were normally distorted beyond recognition and usually too late to do us any good. We began to feel that those at high level were merely trying to prove their superiority, not aid progress on the ground. Frustration prevailed.

By the end of the first winter (the first of three, remember) we saw clearly that hauling horse trailers around the mudded woodlands was not possible. The local ranchers, with the benefit of many years of experience in this landscape, used pickups and trucks fitted with stock racks to reach the lower levels of winter range with their horses. We stayed stuck through much of this winter and accomplished far less than we had hoped.

By spring, we were requesting improved means of moving our horses and dogs. I located in Kanab some slide-in horse racks that would fit our four-wheel-drive vehicles. The cost was $235 each. With relatively simple modifications we could create boxes alongside these racks to handle our dogs. We had welders and necessary tools at Ryan (bought at our own, not the state's expense) to make the modifications. I sent a request to Phoenix for approval to purchase the racks.

After several weeks, while the request traveled upward through all the necessary levels, Phoenix acknowledged the request in principle but stated that the racks would have to be made in the Phoenix shop—three hundred miles from Ryan. We sighed at the absurdity of it all and resignedly delivered one of the two vehicles to Phoenix.

We also delivered detailed sketches of the racks we needed with space for carrying horses and dogs separately. A month later, the vehicle came back with an inadequate metal rack around the bed with no separate compartments for dogs. It was built in a manner that was unsafe for horses, and it would not contain hounds. Tying the dogs so that they could not go over the edge and hang themselves was impossible, and they were not protected from cold and snow. The rack was more useless than the shell camper it had replaced.

Our other vehicle had gone to Phoenix in exchange for the modified one. When I saw the racks, I immediately radioed Phoenix and requested that no work be done on the second rack until we could come down. A week later, we were notified that the second rack was finished. It was as useless as the first. Our heavy work period in the fall was rapidly approaching, so we decided to live with the vehicles as modified. We tried, but they simply wouldn't work. The racks became symbolic of Phoenix's total lack of concern for our needs.

Finally, in desperation, I interrupted the field work and scheduled a week with the welder in Phoenix. We produced a nearly-finished rack that weighed a good two hundred pounds more than the simple ones we had wanted to buy in Kanab. Rather than waste another week in Phoenix, I returned to the Kaibab and had minor work on gates for the rack done at a welding shop in Kanab. The bill was $280.

Modifying the second rack tied up personnel and a vehicle in Phoenix for a second week. The bill at a local shop for finishing the details was only $210 after the truck returned. My exasperation hit a peak, and I wrote a detailed and hostile memo to Phoenix documenting lost time and costs involved in constructing two relatively simple stock racks. When two trips to Phoenix and the costs of two man-weeks per diem in the valley were added to the cost of materials, the price of each rack reached a minimum of $1200. We wasted two weeks of work and burned energy we didn't have to spare. This compares with the $235 cost of the racks we wanted to buy locally.

I was told later by a secretary that a high-level staff member attempted to fire me for insubordination when the memo arrived and that my job was saved by one of my immediate supervisors who claimed that he had asked me to write the memo. Thus the system worked.

Hay for horses was a constant problem on the mountain. We had no pasture, so had to haul in all of the animals' feed. Hay was available in Kanab, thirty miles distant, but we had no storage for it at Ryan. We found ourselves traveling to town almost weekly to buy pickup loads. Hay bought in larger amounts got wet and molded, becoming unfeedable. Buying in such small amounts forced us to pay premium prices, not to mention the cost of gas for the frequent trips.

A simple, cheap solution presented itself. The high school at Fredonia, Arizona, asked me to take on a pair of CETA employees for the summer. They were assigned to me, not the department. I saw an inexpensive labor force for building a hay barn. Pine poles and juniper posts were available on forest lands for the taking. We needed only about $300 in corrugated iron roofing to construct the type of structure present on virtually every ranch in the area. It could be placed near the back of the department's land, thereby being out of sight from the only major road.

My request for galvenized roofing was answered after several weeks with a decision from some five levels up that the new structure would have to be approved by our engineering branch. I sent sketches to Phoenix for approval.

Summer came, and with it my CETA employees. Summer passed and the employees left, having spent their months cleaning the grounds at Ryan and repairing fences. Finally, in November (during the second year of a three-year study, remember) a representative of the construction branch appeared at Ryan with plans for a $17,000 metal building with concrete floor and a single, man-sized walk-in door that would have caused us to carry singly and stack each bale of hay we stored. The construction man was an old timer and was a bit ashamed of the whole thing, but he was only following orders. I pointed out that this structure couldn't possibly be built before the following summer, and considering the slowness of the bid process for such expensive projects, the odds were very high that it would not be built before we finished the study and left. The construction man agreed. I suggested we forget the whole thing. He left. We hauled pickup loads of hay for two more years.

I could tell other, similar stories, but its pointless. The administrators involved at that time are gone. From their own perspectives, they were undoubtedly good people and did good jobs. The point in telling the stories is not to hang dirty linen or to indict individuals. All large organizations have such problems. What is important is the impact on employees—at least those who are trying hard to produce. After a while you cannot help but wonder how decisions are made regarding truly complex situations if simple and relatively clear-cut ones such as these can be so totally botched.

Yet, without the agency, and I suppose, these same administrators, the studies would not have occurred at all. Furthermore, we would have no means to deal with human differences regarding lions or anything else. I'm afraid the process remains an enigma to me.

CHAPTER SIXTEEN
Agencies

 Mount Trumbull overlooks on all sides a vast, relatively uninhabited area known as the Arizona Strip. Its mesa-like top is covered with an uncut stand of ponderosa pine—one of the few such spots remaining in our country. The area surrounding Trumbull, mostly covered with sagebrush or pinyon juniper, is still so uninhabited that, even on a dark night, the view from most points on the mountain's rim will disclose no lights. The few that show will be fifty to sixty miles distant, and the clear air of the southwest allows visibility for a hundred or more. Few remaining places give one a total sense of isolation like Trumbull, and few give one the feeling that humans may still be relatively insignificant on this globe.

I sat on Trumbull during June 1983. I had been assigned by the Arizona Game and Fish Department to make a quick survey of lions on the Arizona Strip because of an impending political flap regarding the condition of the deer herd there. I had found ample lion sign to convince me that lion populations were healthy. My mind was on other matters. I knew lions were there; I suspected that their continued presence was independent of anything humans had or had not done. I wondered how long the human impact could be held back.

My companion was Patty Woodruff, a biologist employed by the Bureau of Reclamation. "Do you believe," I asked her, "looking at the vastness of this land, that agencies, resource managers, or politicians really have anything to do with positive management of wildlands or wildlife?" I expected no answer; she knew the question was rhetorical.

I had recently accompanied Patty to meetings amongst the resource management agencies in Phoenix and had discovered, to my horror, that the main offices of these agencies were housed in a silver-windowed downtown skyscraper. All of my sensibilities recoiled at the thought. I didn't believe that anyone could know, see, or feel resources from such a place. No legitimate decisions could ever be made there. No one who would willingly work in such a place could really value the land.

On Trumbull, this rationale pushed itself further, and I again asked Patty, who was, like me, an employee of the system of conservation, "Do you truly believe that the little knot of people, shuffling papers, making power plays, worrying about intra- and interagency politics, and subsisting in total isolation from the land, really has anything to do with the amount of forage, number of deer, or the future of the lion? Or is it that all a human world unto itself, that is sustained totally for its own existence? Is there a connection between all the urban fuss and bluster and the wilderness?" I was having doubts.

Part of the problem lay in changes in my own thought processes that the act of doing research had created. In studying a species like the lion—to study any species well—you enter its world as fully as possible. You try to break down your personal barriers of culture, upbringing, education, and open your pores to the reality of the creature. You try to see and hear on a subconscious level, continuing to observe even when your mind is otherwise occupied. This is a level of consciousness that modern humans have virtually lost. It has been drilled out of us by way of routine, civilized living, and overconfidence in formal education. When I entered this study, I thought such powers of observation were myths from the days of mountain men. I have since seen them function in old ranchers and old houndsmen. I caught a glimmer of these capabilities in myself, and I liked the feeling.

However, people who have experienced such a connection with nature can never quite again be a part of an agency or organization, nor can they have complete faith in the masses of plans, computer models, meetings, and decisions that daily prevent agency personnel from touching the earth. I believe that a high percentage of those who rise in agencies do so by living intently within the confines of human organization. They do not have time to spend the years necessary to refine the sensitivities of which I speak. And those who enter the trade because they like working in the wilds refuse to sacrifice the high proportion of their life that would be required to ascend in the organization. To them, there is no status in working in the silver-windowed towers.

We therefore have a process of divergence built into our organizations. The good field technician becomes more and more absorbed in the processes of nature knowing that he will never be able to totally agree with the goals of city-bound administrators; the administrator becomes more and more absorbed in the mechanism of the agency, daily trying to make it more efficient and more powerful.

This is the dilemma I have had to confront in dealing with the lion. My sensitivities have been repulsed by the urban world of the agency, but those who control my paycheck and approve the direction of my research are forced to live largely in the other world. They must still believe, or at least pretend to believe, that nature was made for the benefit of humankind. We no longer totally speak the same language. I am not sure that the lions, or wild species in general, are well served.

Nor are all agencies designed to benefit wild species. Government agencies cover the same spectrum in dealing with lions as occurs in the private sector. Each constituency group is represented. The gradient runs from control efforts by Animal Damage Control personnel and Agriculture Extension Agents (both U.S. Department of Agriculture functions), through various levels of efforts at active management of lions by state wildlife departments, to complete protection of national parks and wildlife refuges. Within this array are included the U.S. Forest Service and the Bureau of Land Management—agencies that have generally ignored predators in their management plans but have accidentally been responsible for the continued existence of the lion.

Historically, the Predator and Rodent Control Division of the old U.S. Biological Survey helped exterminate wolves and grizzly bears on the wildlands of the western United States. Had they succeeded, they would willingly have eliminated the coyote and lion as well, but these species proved to be more resilient than other large predators. The vastness of lion habitat, the secretiveness of the species, its resistance to poisoning, and the ability of the lion to recolonize empty habitat rapidly thwarted every effort aimed toward its complete elimination. The lion exists today due to its own invulnerability; not to any altruism on the part of the human species.

The Animal Damage Control Branch still exists, now as a division of the Department of Agriculture, and it continues to deal with lion problems at times. However, it now reacts only to specific cases of livestock depredation by lions, and it limits its efforts to individual animals known to be taking livestock. In the case of losses of range sheep, this approach may be valid. Taking an offending predator from a given mountain pasture may stop losses for a season. It is not, however, a permanent solution, and will probably have to be repeated year after year in the same areas, as new lions replace those removed. The problem will continue as long as sheep are pastured in lion habitat.

Where heavy losses of cattle, mainly calves, occur, taking of the so-called offending lion probably has little value. Our studies on the Spider Ranch indicated that virtually every lion in the area was eating beef. Effective lion control would have required a drastic reduction of the total lion population. Our best evidence suggests that even extremely heavy hunting pressure over a five-year period produced only short term reduction in lion numbers, if in fact a reduction occurred. Under current constraints, lion control by the ADC probably does little to help the range cattle industry.

Wildlife Extension Specialists, also with the Department of Agriculture, have traditionally provided advice and tools to ranchers desiring predator control. This role is gradually changing as better information becomes available to extensionists through research. The present trend is toward recognizing the positive values of predators, either as trophies or furbearers, and encouraging ranchers to incorporate the species into a more holistic approach to land use. Ranchers who realize income from guided hunts for lions usually view the species in a different light than those who see ranching as a cattle or sheep monoculture.

State wildlife agencies tend to represent hunters and fishermen, although their reponsibilities have broadened to include nongame species during recent years. Historically, these agencies advocated predator control, including control of lions, although actual control efforts were usually left to federal ADC people. Acceptance of predators as trophies and fur producers has created regulation of predator harvests via shortened seasons and restricted limits and has reduced predator control support by state game agencies.

Lion regulations vary greatly among states and reflect the extent of losses of livestock and the political strength of the livestock industry. In Texas lions are still considered varmints and receive no legal protection. Arizona has a yearlong season and limits sport hunters to one lion per hunter per year. Ranchers in Arizona are virtually unrestricted in dealing with problems of stock killers. Utah, Colorado, Nevada, Montana, Wyoming, and Idaho use a variety of shortened seasons and limited permit options in controlling lion harvest. At this writing, the lion has been totally protected in California for the past sixteen years.

Interestingly enough, at a recent mountain lion workshop in Zion National Park, biologists from virtually all of the western states claimed stable or increasing lion populations, regardless of the extent of regulation of harvest. The ability of humans to affect lion numbers drastically on western public lands was seriously questioned. In general, lion regulations were designed to satisfy the human populations of the states rather than to accomplish either increases or declines in the numbers of lions.

The greatest problem faced by state agencies in lion management is actual monitoring of lion populations. Estimates of the status of lions in the various states inevitably depend upon harvest data (if hunters are still killing lions, lions must still exist) and upon the opinions of field biologists and conservation officers. The opinions of these field personnel are often derived from information obtained from houndsmen and ranchers. Such information is better than no information at all, but better quantification is badly needed.

One of the myths of wildlife management is that harvest data alone provide adequate monitoring of populations. Modern methods of computer modeling are dispelling this myth and pointing up clearly that harvest data can be extremely misleading if not accompanied by sound surveys of animal numbers and population composition on the ground. Such surveys have long been standard for visible species such as deer, elk, and bighorn sheep. For cryptic species such as lions, bobcats, and bears, field survey techniques have yet to be developed.

The national parks, national wildlife refuges, and, more recently, the state of California protect lions within their boundaries. Few of the refuges are large enough to encompass significant lion populations. Several national parks provide areas large enough to house residual lion populations. These include the Grand Canyon, Carlsbad and Guadalupe Mountains, Zion, Yosemite, Glacier, and Yellowstone. Yellowstone has been a source of puzzlement for its apparent lack of lions. For some reason, complete protection there has not fostered increase of the species, although recent studies have disclosed a good resident population. At the other extreme is the Carlsbad-Guadalupe Mountain area where protected lions range outward from the park and take unattended sheep on ranches around the park's periphery. Continued efforts to control lions here have had virtually no effect.

California protected the lion in 1971. It has been a source of controversy ever since. All indications are that the lion population is healthy in California. Incidence of depredation on livestock has increased over the past ten years, suggesting that that lion population has increased under protection. Incidences of lions in urban areas has also increased, perhaps indicating that the transient age classes of lions are being pushed into more and more marginal habitat. The types of problems this creates have already been discussed. As in other states, California lion regulations reflect the attitude of the human population rather than the status of the wild species.

If California continues to protect lions, the state will undoubtedly provide a reservoir for lions in relatively large parts of western Nevada and southern Oregon. Dispersal into Arizona will probably be minimal due to the severe desert habitats separating Arizona and California.

Perhaps the biggest problem arising from total protection of any species, regardless of the agency involved, is the oft-attending belief that the problems of that species are solved for perpetuity. This may reduce the efforts given to continued monitoring of the animal and eliminates harvest data as a source of information. In the case of predators such as the lion, insidious habitat loss and unreported control efforts may continue, but the mechanisms for monitoring their effects will be lost. All that will remain will be the reports of sensational events such as attacks on humans. In the long run this may be detrimental to the species.

The U.S. Forest Service and the Bureau of Land Management control most of the mountain lion habitat in the United States. Neither of these agencies has historically been involved in lion management. Their policies, however, have favored management of lion prey in the form of deer, elk, cattle, and sheep. They have prevented breaking up of the large expanses of western public lands. This, more than any other human act, has saved the lion. It seems almost ironic that retention of public lands has occurred largely for the benefit of ranchers. There may be a lesson here.

The Forest Service and BLM have traditionally left management of predators on public lands to the interacting forces of ranchers, ADC people, and state wildlife agencies. At the same time, they probably have had the best tools available to ease some of the stresses of the lion issue through modification of grazing fee structures, controlling types of livestock operations, and manipulation of habitat. Grazing fees constitute a significant portion of the overhead of working ranches (at present, on the order of 20 percent of gross). Efforts are afoot to make such fees even larger. Neither agency involved in administering these fees recognizes the differential problems of ranching in their fee structure. Ranchers in areas with histories of high predator losses pay the same grazing fee per head as those in areas where predation is insignificant. The predator problem is a factor of habitat types. A sliding fee structure would acknowledge this and reduce the economic stress on ranchers in high predation areas. Inherent in this system, of course, would be agreements by ranchers to cease predator control and to accept predation as part of the cost of doing business. Adequate penalties to enforce these provisions would be needed.

Our work on the Spider Ranch and subsequent interviews of ranchers have demonstrated that the greatest impacts of lions on cattle occur where calves are raised in areas with high lion densities. Avoiding cow-calf operations in good lion country, or structuring allotments to allow calf-rearing out of lion country could alleviate much of the lion problem. Losses are greatly reduced once calves reach five to six months of age.

High lion densities, hence lion-cattle problems, occur mainly in the brushy habitats of the central and southern Arizona mountains. Lions seem to survive better, perhaps stalk better, in the denser cover. Fire control measures of the USFS and BLM have favored encroachment of dense chaparral and other vegetation, thereby encouraging increase of lion predation. Although prescribed burning is becoming more widely accepted in these habitats, land managers are still conservative in its use. They tend to burn small tracts where high levels of control can be maintained. Fairly large burns, in the twenty thousand-acre category or larger, could modify habitat use patterns of lions and provide areas of sanctuary for both cattle and deer.

Enhancing the trophy value of the lion via support of good guiding operations may have merit in lion management. The Forest Service has recently entered this arena of management by initiating a program of increased fees and increased regulation of guides operating on forest lands. This may be detrimental to guides initially, but it could be used to elevate standards of guiding as a business. If it accomplishes nothing else, it seems to be causing guides to unite into organizations and to become a stronger political force. In the end, this may create an improvement in guiding ethics and involve guides more fully in managing the species that they help to consume.

CHAPTER SEVENTEEN
Hopes, Fears, and Pleas

 I hoped when I began writing this book (now almost ten years ago) that I could pick up a thread of belief in the system that would reverse my seemingly negative trend of thought. If so, this final chapter could be a chapter of fanfare with recommendations for redirection of agencies involved with the lion. I hoped that, if I pulled together an overview of the knowledge I had gained working on lions, the feelings I had developed, and the insights I had formed regarding others interested in the lion, the result would be a synthesis that would help end the conflicts surrounding the species once and for all. In so doing, it could give a glimmer of the future—the other half of the cougar equation. We all get our doses of megalomania.

Such a clear insight hasn't happened. I've ended instead with an acknowledgement of the conflict and the reality of its biological basis. I've also developed fears that the different viewpoints may be relatively constant in our culture, not necessarily to be changed by facts.

Lions do, at least in places, compete with ranchers and deer hunters. At present, as a species, lions apparently are not threatened in the western U.S., western Canada, and (although little is known there) much of Latin America. For the short run, their future seems intact.

In dealing with the lion, I hope that we are in a time of changing directions. In the annals of human endeavor, the predator eradication era has apparently ended. With luck, it will not start again. The wolf in most of the West succumbed to this era; the grizzly bear nearly so, at least in the lower 48. The lion, coyote, and black bear have withstood everything humans have been able to throw at them, and they have survived. They are now expanding their range. To me this is a sign of hope.

Also, in dealing with the lion, we are (again in the slow ebb of human history) at the beginning of an era in which humans may reassess their role on earth. We have assumed to this time—our religions have taught us to this time—that all of nature was designed to serve us. It was put here for our use. I hope we are learning greater humility. However impressive our technological advances, we have made almost no gain in our abilities to avoid war and other forms of human violence. In fact, our increasing human populations and our technology seem to add to our capacity for violence. In the sense that we cannot control our own propensity to destroy, and in the sense that we are as dependent upon natural food chains as all other life on earth, we must come to humbly view ourselves as just another species, albeit a complex one.

The great environmental thrust of the seventies is over. Its end was inevitable. No culture can focus that much energy on an issue forever. Life goes on and other problems demand attention. Nonetheless, that environmental thrust had its impact. Important regulations were passed during that era, but these, in reality, are temporary. They are merely the symbols that caused us to pause and think for a decade. Each new administration shows us emphatically that such laws can be politically modified and chipped away.

More important than laws are the human products of the environmental era, now entering the world of commerce. We seem to be in a surge of industrialization again. Our young people are wearing grey flannel suits and looking disgustingly respectable. But buried within these youngsters are the vestiges of an awareness created in the seventies—and in the midst of their acquisitiveness, I hope that they know, better than their grandparents did, the cost of their consumption to the land.

If we consider our increasing realization, due to modern astronomy, that our earth with all of its living creatures, is a rarity in the Universe—rarer than the rarest of endangered species—perhaps we can begin to develop a real compassion for what we are. We are, as a planet, one in billions. With all of the effort directed toward space research during this century, we have as yet no indication that any other planet anywhere has produced the variety of life forms found on earth. We are an oasis in infinity. We are rarer than the rarest of anything that one can conceive, when viewed on a universal scale. The extent to which we reduce the variety of life on this planet, the extent to which we simplify it to suit our own needs, is equally the extent to which we approach the same status of the many dead worlds that surround us. We would do well to daily impose this scale of things upon our consciousness.

However, we must also consider the alternate interpretation. We are so small in this universe that our planet is insignificant. Even though we, and the lion, focus all of the forces of nature into our genetic and cultural inheritances, even if we are each an equal sign in some ecological equation, we are physically the center of nothing. The universe would not miss the planet Earth. It will not miss lions. It will not miss humans. What we believe relative to predator management is, in the grand scale, inconsequential. Most of the ethical proclamations we impose upon our fellow humans, including those dealing with predator control or hunting, merely reflect our inner wants, not moral absolutes. The word "should" is a manipulative device and members of our species, especially those that profess to lead, are all too adept at using it to convert their personal desires and anxieties into moral edicts. Thus, I refuse to use the technical information gathered on lions to moralize on lion management.

At present, our relationships with all wild species suffer from an analog of the phenomenon of racism carried to the species level. It's called anthropocentricity. Nearly all human cultures have some special name for themselves that usually interprets to mean "the people." Other cultures are generally considered to be something inferior. Perhaps one of the most positive attributes of modern humans is the effort to combat such notions. We continue, however, to assume without question our superiority to other species. Our technology is our evidence to support this assumption. After I had been close to the lion, the same technology became a sign of weakness. Consider the beast that lives on the land, feeds itself by killing the fleetest of animals without using weapons, and survives the severest of weather without any of the technological crutches that we see as necessities. In the niche of the lion, we are not its superior, and it deserves a certain awe.

I would like to believe that our agencies increasingly promote people who have this kind of awe, but my hope really lies more with those of whom I have written and seemingly criticized—guides, ranchers, hunters, preservationists, and the field biologists. These often seem to be opposed to each other, but they exist at the grass roots. And it is here that changes, to be effective, must be made, not in the abstract world of silver-windowed towers and paper.

I can't predict the future of the lion. For the present, I'm convinced that as long as we have large expanses of wild lands that cannot be settled, the lion will exist. I'm also convinced that it is the interactions of these groups that will assure the continued existence of wildlands, hence wild species. If they do their part well, the agencies, designed to follow, must follow. I hope that no single interest group gains excessive power. This applies especially to government personnel. And I am one of those.

To end, then, although I won't moralize on lion management, I will express my wants, as one who likes lions, to those others who value wildness for whatever reason.

To the lion hunters and guides, we need your help in nurturing the species you consume. The day of killing lions as a heroic deed is past. Contribute to our awareness and help us to keep the wild, western public lands so essential to this species. Value it as the ultimate, pristine trophy that it is.

To the rancher, I wish you could respect the cat a bit more. Your habitats are the same. You could seek extinction together. Acknowledge yourself as a fellow species and adjust your operation rather than seeking total control of your environment. In the annals of the human species, control and destruction are synonymous. Whatever the goals of your ancestors, you no longer need to tame the frontier.

To the deer hunter, please try to value wildness for wildness' sake. If you eliminate lions for the purpose of making your deer hunting easy, you've reduced your own value as a hunter. You've moved one step closer to herding sheep. Each step toward domestication is a step away from true wildness. And there is little enough of that left as it is.

To the preservationist, please be careful in your quest for regulation. You place too much trust in these symbols of the system and their agencies. Yours will be paper victories enforced by paper people. They lead to complacency and reduced awareness in the end. Your real allies are the ranchers and the hunters. They, too, value the land.

To the biologist, stay on the land until you are secure in your inner connections with nature. Don't be deluded into thinking that uniform policies, management plans, and personnel regulations supercede natural law. Focus your attention on what is really happening to species, and be wary of complex administrative plans to be superimposed on nature. They are as ephemeral as the administrations that create them.

And to the lion—and the hounds—we know you won't change, but hang in there. At least some of us want very much to keep you around.

About the Author

Harley Shaw claims to be a native of both Arizona and Oklahoma. His father was working on Bartlett Dam when he was conceived, and his mother returned to her native Oklahoma for his birth. He grew up in Arizona. He started with the Arizona Game and Fish Department during his first summer out of Tempe Union High School, in 1955. He completed a B.S. degree in wildlife management at the University of Arizona and an M.S. degree in wildlife management at the University of Idaho. From 1963 to 1990, he worked as a research biologist for the Arizona Game and Fish Department, carrying out projects on mule deer, wild turkeys, mountain lions, and desert bighorns. Shaw spent eight years capturing and radio-tracking mountain lions near Prescott and in the north Kaibab National Forest. His work on lions led to publication of *A Mountain Lion Field Guide*, recently updated by The Cougar Network with contributions by several new authors. He has authored and co-authored articles on mountain lions in *The Journal of Wildlife Management* and various symposia and proceedings. He hosted the Third Mountain Lion Workshop in Prescott, Arizona. He was on the team that wrote and published the *First Cougar Management Guidelines* and has more recently authored a chapter on cougar research history in *Cougar Ecology and Conservation*.

Since retiring, Shaw has continued to write and do research. In 2001, he and his wife, Patty Woodruff, moved to Hillsboro, New Mexico. In 2004, the University of Arizona Press published *Stalking the Big Bird*, which tells of his work with the Merriam's wild turkey in northern Arizona. Other works include *Garden Canyon Watershed, a Vision and a Mission*, written for the U.S. Army at Fort Huachuca; *Wood Plenty, Grass Good, Water None: Featuring Twenty-three Days with Lieutenant Amiel Weeks Whipple in His 1854 Exploration of the Upper Verde Watershed*; and *Natural History of a Small Place: A Landscape History of Pueblo Colorado Wash at Hubbell Trading Post*. Since moving to New Mexico, Shaw has hosted four mountain lion field workshops on Ted Turner's Ladder Ranch, which have been attended by wildlife biologists from midwestern and eastern states, Canadian provinces, and Australia. He recently completed a book on the early career of New Mexico biologist J. Stokley Ligon, which will be published by the University of Arizona Press in 2011. He has served in an advisory capacity on mountain lion and bighorn studies on Ladder and Armendaris Ranches and is currently working on an ecological history of goat ranching in the Black Range of New Mexico.